AF395149

THE NATURE & KINDS OF AUTISM INCLUDING ASPERGER'S SYNDROME

A deep understanding of Autism and Asperger's differences and causes.
How to manage kids and adults with the syndrome and prevent it

Selva Sugunendran

CEng, MIEE, MCMI, CHt, MIMDHA, MBBNLP, MABNLP
#1 Best Selling Author, Speaker & Coach

FOREWORD

ttending to persons with regular diseases and pathologies has been more like waking up every new day and going to check on the mirror how old you have become. Here, we are going to do more than just checking the wrinkles - by exploring every detail to tell whether or not our judgment is worth it.

So, are you a friend or colleague of someone whose child seems a bit different than most people? They may have shared with you how they're autistic, or "on the spectrum". You might have been surprised, as they don't fit that stereotypical image of an autistic person. And if you have a child who's recently been diagnosed, or you're an adult who suspects you may be autistic, this book will help you to better understand the condition, how it doesn't change your relationship with family, coworkers, or work colleagues. Remember they trusted you with this important aspect of their lives as well as they too need to know and learn to tolerate your caprices should you be autistic.

Adding to the facts elaborated here by Selva, the statistics for how many people in the world have autism can vary. Some will say 2% of our population is born autistic. In fact, a person is born with autism as this isn't a condition that you can "catch" like a cold or flu bug. If we include all types of neurodiversity, up to 15% of the world's population may have a challenging developmental condition.

In many parts of the world, the term "Asperger's" is no longer used. All autistic people are simply "autistic". It's also acceptable to say, "on the spectrum" or "neurodiverse".

As you will read, autism can affect both the body and the mind, and for this reason, it's called a developmental condition for babies and young children, that can also affect them into adulthood. Parents are often worried when their child receives an autistic diagnosis, but please don't be, as the autistic person may have challenges, but they're still human beings.

Two autistic people placed side by side can be as different as anyone else. If you've watched TV programs or films with autistic people, what you'll see is a stereotypical version of an autistic person. Not all autistic people are cold calculating geniuses. There are plenty of myths surrounding autistic people, such as they're not empathetic, which isn't always true. In fact, autistic people can possess high levels of empathy that can lead to mental breakdowns as the brain is over-processing. Just like the genome of the human being, everyone is different.

There are DNA tests that may or may not detect autism in your child. Right now, scientists are learning more and more about what it really is. If you choose to have the DNA test done for your child and get a positive diagnosis, then that's fantastic, you're one step closer to helping them out. If the test comes back as negative, that doesn't mean that they aren't autistic. It's simply a diagnostic tool that may or may not work. There are also many other diagnostic tools that the psychologist or psychiatrist may use to diagnose you or your child.

As they say in Cameroon, a kid can never look like an ewe. Often if a child is autistic, the experts say, "Look to the parents and family members". Because chances are that one of them is also autistic. There probably are thousands of adults who survived childhood and are autistic, but have never been diagnosed. This is especially true of women, because of the way they are trained differently as young girls. And again, some children in the past may have experienced child abuse when their parents couldn't figure out why there was a temper tantrum or mental breakdown and would use violence to get them to stop.

Just like the ingredients that make up pizza, autism involves being diagnosed with several different conditions. All grouped together, it can make life a challenge for this person. For example, being mute, having sensory disorders, having ADHD, dyslexia, and other health or mental conditions can give a person a positive autistic diagnosis. Some people have only one issue, such as ADHD or dyslexia, but it will not give them an autistic diagnosis because it's only one challenge in life.

No hungry man would like to remain hungry for life - If there's one thing that autistic people would like everyone to know, it's that they don't want their autism to be "fixed". Can you imagine if you had to deal with these prejudices your entire life and be told something is wrong with you? This would cause you to mask (hide your condition), and that can be harmful if you do it for long lengths of time.

Pre-1990s, children of all abilities were placed into the same classrooms. Even now you might remember a classmate who had difficulties concentrating, or would be muttering or stimming (repetitive sounds or movements to help concentrate). We just accepted our classmates back then.

Today, neurodiverse children are placed into separate classrooms. Sometimes these classrooms offer certain types of therapy, such as "ABA" (Applied Behaviour Analysis) that can be abusive when bad behaviour is punished. But the good news is that we continue to learn and improve supportive programs for people on the spectrum.

It's believed that autism may have been more prevalent during the times of early humans in history. The reason is that people with heightened sensory abilities would be the ones who would survive, while others without would become food for predators, or eat something poisonous. This is another reason why many autistic people today feel they don't need to be "fixed", but that human life has evolved so much that now they must adapt to the modern world.

With the humanity built in us, autistic people do need our help in managing the challenges they face. Challenges with social interaction, ADHD, sensory issues, education, finding jobs, and more, will cause an autistic person to break down and need help from a professional, as well as understanding from the people surrounding them.

Why must an orange become an apple and not the other way round? It's important to understand that autistic people may have some resentment. After all, why should they adapt to certain situations? Why can't people adapt to them? Today, many stores are offering a special day when neurodiverse people can enter their shops and enjoy decreased lighting levels, no music or announcements, and decreased activity from staff. Isn't that fantastic that people will adapt so your autistic child will have a great day?

I enjoyed reading Selva's book very much. I hope you too will enjoy reading this well researched and beautifully presented facts in a very easily understood format and learning more about this condition. Once you open your heart to your autistic friends, family, and colleagues, you'll discover how you want to assist them in living happy and healthy lives, rather than trying to "fix them".

Agnes Waters

DEDICATION

This book is dedicated to those who wish to learn about Autism Spectrum disorder (including Asperger's syndrome), as well as those who have just noticed the symptoms or received a diagnosis for their child, to show that there is hope.

ABOUT THE AUTHOR

Selva Sugunendran built a successful U.K. based IT company. After twenty-five years at the helm, he sold his business to pursue a greater, more meaningful passion: helping others find success. Since leaving his company, he has inspired countless people from all walks of life to recognise their strengths and help them hone in on them to find their own paths to success in life and business. He's also expanded his reach by penning multiple books, chapters, and guest posts that spread his proven ideology and methods for individual growth for people of all ages.

Named an Expert Platinum Author, his work has afforded him opportunities to meet and work with people of all ages and learn first-hand what they need to achieve optimal success. One such area that captured his interest is the plight of those living with what is considered to be incurable health issues. Since obtaining a University Diploma in dementia and some considerable research, he has published five books on dementia based on scientific and medical research. Subsequently, he has also published two books based on spiritual truths for all those in an advanced state of such diseases.

This book is a result of working closely with a number of parents (and close family members/ friends) of children diagnosed in the autistic spectrum, including Asperger's syndrome. This book is designed to help them understand what this condition is and how the diagnosed child can be helped to live as much a "normal life "as possible, depending on where in the autistic spectrum the child is.

When not writing or researching, Selva can be found exploring new ways to lift others up and help them live the life of their dreams.

ACKNOWLEDGEMENT

During the last two years of active research into the autistic spectrum including Asperger's syndrome, my knowledge has been enriched by so many people who have given their time, research, experiences, opinions and wisdom.

Unfortunately, there is not enough room here to acknowledge each and every one of them. My special heartful thanks go to all those kind people.

Thanks also to my wife Kamini, my son Shaun, daughter(in-law) Florence Nishanthi and my two grandchildren Jason & Lisa, for their support and understanding as I spent long hours researching and travelling to gather the data required to write this book.

I would also like to thank those who have inspired me, including Rex Thorne, Alan Clasby, Pastors T.U. Thomas, Ranjit, Ernest Paul and Rudran.

My heartful thanks also go to those that I couldn't mention. You know who you are!

I cannot end this acknowledgment without giving thanks to God, who has provided me with everything I need, as illustrated in Philippines 4: Verses 11-13

Why I wrote this Book

Due to my experience in charity organisations and quest for reaching out to those in greatest need, every disease that does not have a human cure attracts my attention, and this time, Autism Spectrum Disorder falls into this category.

Therefore, I decided to research, discuss and explore to bring to light as much information about this disease, considering that this knowledge can be of great help to those with symptoms or diagnosed with this disease as well as those caring for them.

Why you should read this book

As humans, we are called to be each other's keeper. This book gives us insight into how to recognise and take care of our loved ones or any other humans suffering from autism spectrum disorder or any other health disorder life may present us with. Equally, this book will enlighten anyone suffering from the aforementioned disorder and help pave the way for better self-management and ensure that any children do not suffer the same.

TABLE OF CONTENTS

PART I

Introduction

This book is written to inform about Autism and Asperger's syndrome. Autism was first diagnosed by Dr. Leo Kanner at John Hopkins Hospital in 1942, and Asperger's syndrome was recognised by Hans Asperger, a Viennese pediatrician in the 1940s, though history shows that these disorders had existed long before the 20th century. Considering the growth in cases of these health impairments in our society today, I found it necessary to create more awareness by using different words to express the intricacies surrounding these conditions. Therefore, I am not discounting what other writers have highlighted but align behind them to reach the maximum population possible. Taking into account the perception of the general public towards the guardians and patients of these health conditions, it rings an alarm for a better sensitization of the masses to better cohabit and understand each other. At some point in this book, Asperger's syndrome will not be treated separately from Autism.

Layman's definition of Autism and Asperger's syndrome

Asperger's Syndrome

My neighbor's child had difficulties talking at the age of 2. He would seldom smile back at us but preferred being in one corner all by himself and repeatedly nodding his head. Donald would not find interest in picking up a pen and writing like my 20-month old twin liked to do. Though he was good at building beautiful castles with the bricks he owned, Donald's father, a coworker at a local factory, told me that Donald was suffering from Asperger's syndrome. Asperger's syndrome means that Donald can't handle certain tasks or respond to certain signals due to a slower behavioural response to a lesser extent. Donald needed to be followed up closely as well as given an adapted form of education that would adequately nurture the impaired part of him. Nonetheless, his friends would need to learn to appreciate him the way he is.

Autism

Donald's father equally told me that in the course of his numerous appointments with the children's doctor, he'd met some cases worse than his son, which the doctor called autism. These cases, he said, are children who had difficulties not only in speech and writing but could not even build castles as Donald would. They would sometimes barely move a muscle when being spoken to. Others even hurt themselves in the course of repeatedly scratching their scalp. He equally said there was a school meant for children like Donald and other elderly people who had not had the opportunity to go to school but had been living with the disability.

Scientific definition of Autism & Asperger's syndrome

Asperger's syndrome

Asperger's syndrome is a shade on the autism spectrum, with generally higher functioning. Higher functioning means the individual has a higher IQ or better interactive responses compared to a full degree autistic. This disorder is equally characterised by significant difficulties in socialization and verbal communication. Like autism, the individual equally has restricted and repetitive behavioural patterns and interests. In this case, it is as though we are considering the Autism Spectrum from 1 to 5, and Asperger's syndrome falls at the value of 2. As mentioned earlier, autistics generally have issues with communication as well as understanding what other people think or feel. Due to these inabilities, they cannot express themselves by gesticulation, facial expressions or touch. From the National Institute of Mental Health (NIH), *"Asperger syndrome (AS) is a developmental disorder. It is an autism spectrum disorder (ASD), one of a distinct group of neurological conditions characterised by a greater or lesser degree of impairment in language and communication skills, as well as repetitive or restrictive patterns of thought and behaviour. Other ASDs include: classic autism, Rett syndrome, childhood disintegrative disorder, and pervasive developmental disorder not otherwise specified (usually referred to as PDD-NOS). Unlike children with autism, children with AS retain their early language skills.*

The most distinguishing symptom of AS is a child's obsessive interest in a single object or topic to the exclusion of any other. Children with AS want to know everything about their topic of interest, and their conversations with others will be about little else. Their expertise, high level of vocabulary, and formal speech patterns make them seem like little professors. Other characteristics of AS include repetitive routines or rituals; peculiarities in speech and language; socially and emotionally inappropriate behaviour and the inability to interact successfully with peers; problems with non-verbal communication; and clumsy and uncoordinated motor movements.

Children with AS are isolated because of their poor social skills and narrow interests. They may approach other people, but make normal conversation impossible by inappropriate or eccentric behaviour, or by wanting only to talk about their singular interest. Children with AS usually have a history of developmental delays in motor skills, such as pedaling a bike, catching a ball, or climbing outdoor play equipment. They are often awkward and poorly coordinated with a walk that can appear either stilted or bouncy."

Autism

Autism is a scale of neuropsychiatric disorders marked by a lack of socialisation and communication, as well as an unusual repetitive or unchanging pattern of behaviour.

It can equally be called autism spectrum disorder (ASD), which takes into consideration a wide range of symptoms and skills. A person affected by autism is called an autistic. This disorder can be minor and can solicit pretty much attention depending on the severity. In this case, special homes or facilities will be required to take care of the individual involved.

The National Institute of Mental Health (NIH) says, *"Autism spectrum disorder (ASD) is a developmental disorder that affects communication and behaviour. Although autism can be diagnosed at any age, it is said to be a "developmental disorder" because symptoms generally appear in the first two years of life."*

According to the Diagnostic and Statistical Manual of Mental Disorders (DSM-5), a guide created by the American Psychiatric Association used to diagnose mental disorders, people with ASD have:

- *Difficulty with communication and interaction with other people*

- *Restricted interests and repetitive behaviours*

- *Symptoms that hurt the person's ability to function properly in school, work, and other areas of life.*

Autism is known as a "spectrum" disorder because there is wide variation in the type and severity of symptoms people experience. ASD occurs in all ethnic, racial, and economic groups. Although ASD can be a lifelong disorder, treatments and services can improve a person's symptoms and ability to function. The American Academy of Pediatrics recommends that all children be screened for autism. All caregivers should talk to their doctor about ASD screening or evaluation.

They may find it difficult to learn or develop skills evenly. As seen in the layman's definition above, some autistics may have issues with communication but are pretty good when it comes to playing music, drawing, construction, solving equations and even memorizing things. Due to this, they may perform extremely well when it comes to solving practical problems.

Most often, one cannot easily distinguish a normal individual from an autistic. The easier ways to know is the difference in communication, social interaction, behavioural pattern and pace in the acquisition of knowledge or skills. Even though 30-50% of people with autism have seizures, uncertainty lies with the remaining 50-70%.

In 1943, Dr. Leo Kanner defined autism as a visible lack of interest in other people but an unusually heightened interest in inanimate objects. This was based on some 11 children whom he monitored. Autism was first believed to be an earlier form of schizophrenia whose origin can be due to poor parenting or a traumatizing experience. Based on the wide knowledge we have acquired to this day, we can freely debunk this belief.

In the course of exploring the findings elaborated in this book, it will be important to note that ASD, in most places, will enclose Asperger's syndrome.

According to neurologists and other specialists involved in the identification and management of autistic disorder, ASD can be classified into five different types according to severity. Following an increasing trend of severity, we have;

- **Asperger's syndrome (AS)**

As defined above, it is the least autistic disorder in terms of severity of mental impairment. A person with AS is thus closest to a normal functioning individual than any other in the autistic umbrella.

- **Pervasive Developmental Disorder – Not Otherwise Specified (PDD – NOS)**

It is like autism, a neuro-developmental disorder, which hinders the growth and development of the brain. Out of the various shades of autism, diagnosing specialists consider PDD-NOS non-typical autism; this is because persons diagnosed with this condition often do not display the typical criteria normally expressed by individuals with classical autism.

• Childhood Disintegrative Disorder (CDD)

This disorder was diagnosed and documented in 1908 by Theodor Heller, an erstwhile Austrian Educator. His observation was that CDD is a multifaceted disorder affecting many complex areas of a child's development. It wasn't until 1994 that this disorder was considered a mental health issue, not a medical problem; thus, it was classified under the autism spectrum. It then initiated the appellation of *Heller's syndrome* in children. This is an extremely rare condition in which children develop normally up to the age of about 24 months and then suffer a severe loss of social, behavioural and communication skills. Childhood Disintegrative Disorder is sometimes referred to as *Dementia Infantilis* or *Disintegrative Psychosis* with a rare occurrence of 1 child out of 100,000 children. Just like most autistic disorders, it occurs 4 times in males than in female children.

• Rett Syndrome

Rett syndrome is a neurodevelopmental disorder that almost exclusively affects female children. Children with Rett syndrome, in the initial stages, tend to portray symptoms that are very much likened to early signs of autism. Much like autism, children with this disorder show normal growth and development followed by a gradual or sudden regression of their developmental skills.

Most children diagnosed with this syndrome will have slower head and brain growth, which is often an early sign of the disorder. Seizures are pretty common as well. Rett syndrome is the rarest among the major types of autism and perhaps the only one that could be confirmed with the help of medical tests. The support level required for female children with Rett's syndrome ranges from Level 2 to Level 3. (The support levels are rated 1 to 3 according to severity of the autistic disorder).

- **Classical Autism**

This is defined as the most severe form of autistic spectrum disorder. It is also known as 'severe autism,' 'Kanner's syndrome' and 'autism disorder.' Here, we observe extreme and most impaired abilities from the normal behavioural trend. Therefore, this requires Level 3 support, and this is what we are going to handle extensively in this book.

Symptoms of Autism and Asperger's syndrome

Symptoms of Autism

In considering the lack of a square-cut diagnosis for ASD, there are symptoms to prove this disorder. Autistics either have a similar appearance or are thought to be caused by the same underlying mechanism. There's no particular age for someone to start showing symptoms of autism; however, from twelve months when a baby starts presenting distinct growth in mobility and speech, a parent might start getting warning signs. Parents should always be watchful and observant to spot any abnormality so that right and conscious choices can be made as early as possible. Having said this, there are quite a handful of red lights indicative of autism in a child. Below is a cross-section of these symptoms.

Autism particularly affects a person's perception as well as socialization. An autistic will tend not to mingle among his own age group or any other age group. However, he chooses one thing and does it over and over again. For instance, if his own means of catching fun is by playing a particular game, then he'll play that same game without changing to any other. Ordinarily, this should become very boring to a child, as children tend to easily get captured by any new thing which comes their way. If you have other children in the house, you'll notice they will start avoiding playing with this child after a brief moment of play; meanwhile, he'll keep on and on. This should make an observant parent begin to raise eyebrows.

Also, a person with autism tends to stick to patterns. This is often related to food and sleep. If his pattern is waking up to brush and eat, then breaking or disrupting this pattern can provoke agitation or even revolt. He expects that things should always be done in the same pattern. However, it is important to know that not everybody who follows a pattern in life is autistic. Some people, autistic or not, may still follow a pattern in life due to their lifestyle or other reasons. Therefore, this means that one should not immediately conclude a child's health state simply because he follows a pattern in his life. There is a difference. An autistic will greatly revolt upon a change of pattern while others might just worry without physically getting agitated. One should be very careful while following up a child to detect his state because children will generally stick to a pattern, especially when feeding is involved. So upon observing, use several other things and not just feeding. A naughty child might even roll on the floor simply because of food in the morning. He might refuse to brush because he wants to eat, while an autistic will revolt because you want him to eat before brushing. That's how much they stick to patterns.

A child with autism will almost never look at someone in the face as he talks to them. He'll look anywhere else than into the face of someone trying to communicate with them. Eye contact happens to be impossible with them. They do not just look away like someone shy, so one should not make a mistake here. They look in different directions, especially with bowed and unsteady heads.

Sometimes, some of them will not respond to their names when called. When a parent or care taker calls, and a child does not acknowledge most of the time, making it seem like he does not recognise his name. That should begin to serve as an eye-opener. However, some children could refuse to answer to their names out of sheer naughtiness. This could just happen once, but if this behaviour becomes recurrent, then watch out as this could possibly be an indicator of autism.

Kings is a friend's autistic son. Sometimes, if not most times, he tends to behave indifferently towards his parents, same as his caregiver. He ignores them when spoken to. Worst of all, when he's asked a question, look around in case it's someone else they are talking to because sometimes he simply does not respond at all. He ignores them completely. This is another indicator of autism.

Most autistic children will behave like they are emotionally detached. They don't seem to care for those around them or about the emotional changes of those around them. Some parents blackmail their children by faking to cry. This naturally makes children want to do favours so that their loved ones do not cry. This trick will seldom work for an autistic child. These emotional changes tend to mean little to them and rather keeps them uncomfortable. However, this particular symptom is not common with all autistic children.

In addition, some children develop normally in speech, but suddenly, this starts failing after about two years. Speech defects are a predominant challenge with autistic children, so once a child starts to lose his ability to communicate verbally, it's a cause for concern. Other factors besides autism could be advanced for a child losing his speech, but this does not rule out autism.

Some autistic children tend to be withdrawn. This could be from a slightly advanced age in the child's later days or from birth, meaning you start noticing it as they grow up. Most autistic children may start withdrawing from about two years and above. At some point, they even tend to be aggressive if someone attempts touching or simply comes close to them.

These are other red lights indicating the presence of autism in a child. Note that it's not too long before the symptoms start presenting themselves. In most cases, these begin as early as a couple of months. Nevertheless, parents should never draw a conclusion without visiting the hospital for a proper diagnosis.

Symptoms of Asperger's syndrome

Like autism, Asperger's has no particular symptom since no two children with the disorder are likely to present the same symptoms. Some individuals may have minor issues, which do hinder their normal daily life, while others will find it difficult to succeed academically, socially or even at the job site.

It remains primordial to know the different symptoms because they will help parents and patients to get a better diagnosis.

According to Everyday Health, they classify symptoms into Social, Language and speech, Cognitive and Physical and define them as follows:

Social Symptoms

One telltale sign of Asperger's syndrome is having difficulty in social situations.

Common symptoms of Asperger's that may impact social interaction or communication include:

- Problems making or maintaining friendships
- Isolation or minimal interaction in social situations
- Poor eye contact or the tendency to stare at others
- Trouble interpreting gestures
- Inability to recognise humor, irony, and sarcasm
- Inappropriate behaviours or odd mannerisms
- Problems expressing empathy, controlling emotions, or communicating feelings
- Lack of common sense
- Tendency to engage in one-sided conversations (about oneself)
- Fascination with certain topics
- Interpretation of information as literal
- The preference for a strict schedule or routine

An adult or child with Asperger's may not show all these signs, but, in general, tends to struggle in social situations.

Some people might interpret a child's symptoms as simply rude behaviour. For instance, individuals with Asperger's might talk exclusively about themselves. They may not recognise when someone is uncomfortable, disinterested, or offended. Because they don't always recognise social cues, they may speak loudly at inappropriate times, such as during a church service.

A person with Asperger's might talk obsessively about one particular subject. For example, he or she might be able to recite different types of flowers or sports statistics.

Language and Speech Issues

Unlike other autism spectrum disorders, a person with Asperger's typically doesn't experience a speech delay. But they do have specific language behaviours that set them apart.

A child or adult with Asperger's may exhibit the following:

- A scripted, formal, or "robotic" type of speaking
- Lack of inflection when talking
- Repetitive speech
- Trouble using language in a social context
- Loud or high-pitched speech

Individuals with Asperger's typically have an advanced vocabulary and good grammar skills but might not be able to use language appropriately in social situations.

To an outsider, the speech pattern of a child with Asperger's may sound unusual. They may speak in a very monotone or rhythmic manner, with a loud voice.

Cognitive Behaviours

Typically, kids and adults with Asperger's have normal to above-average intelligence. While some excel academically, others might struggle.

Some common cognitive traits in people with Asperger's include:

- A superior rote memory
- Ability to understand technical or factual information
- Trouble absorbing abstract information
- Tendency to focus on details, which may result in missing "the bigger picture"

Children with Asperger's might experience trouble focusing or have a nonverbal associated learning disability that can affect their reading, writing, or math skills. Still, many don't have any cognitive issues.

Physical Symptoms

Kids with Asperger's might experience physical symptoms, such as:

- Delay in motor skills
- Awkward movements
- Problems with coordination
- Sensitivity to loud noises, odors, clothing, or food textures

Children with Asperger's may appear clumsy or awkward. They might have trouble with simple activities, such as catching a ball or swinging on monkey bars at a playground. However, some kids don't have any motor skill problems.

Diagnosis of Autism and Asperger's syndrome

Diagnosing autism spectrum disorder (ASD) can be pretty difficult because there is no well-established medical test, like a blood test or tissue analysis to diagnose the disorder. Instead, doctors emphasise the child's developmental history and behavioural pattern obtained either from their parents or guardians to make a diagnosis. Generally, ASD can sometimes be detected at 18 months or less. Some experts say there is no particular age to start expressing the conditions. In all, early diagnosis is the only way to make a great difference in the lives of autistics and their families as well. Autism is first diagnosed by a pediatrician. Between the 18 and 24th month after birth, the child needs to be assessed and the right decisions made if he presents any symptoms.

In the course of these visits, the pediatrician will watch the child and talk to him. Then ask questions to the parent or guardian about the child's development and behaviour as well as family history (to know if any family member is in some way in the autism spectrum).

The pediatrician may ask the following leading questions:

Does the child have repetitive and unusual behaviour?

- Is the child having issues with making eye contact?
- Did the child mimic facial expressions and sounds by 9 months?
- Did the child babble and coo by 12 months?
- Did the baby smile by 6 months?
- Does the child interact with people?
- Does he respond when someone wants his attention?
- Does the child get angry often?
- Is the child sensitive to temperature, light and noise?
- Does the child have issues with sleep and digestion?
- What is the child's voice tone? Flat?

According to NIMH, they classify diagnosis as follows:

Doctors diagnose ASD by looking at a person's behaviour and development. ASD can usually be reliably diagnosed by the age of two. It is important for those with concerns to seek out assessment as soon as possible so that a diagnosis can be made, and treatment can begin.

Diagnosis in Young Children

Diagnosis in young children is often a two-stage process.

Stage 1: General Developmental Screening During Well-Child Checkups

Every child should receive well-child check-ups with a pediatrician or an early childhood health care provider. The American Academy of Pediatrics recommends that all children be screened for developmental delays at their 9-, 18-, and 24- or 30-month well-child visits and specifically for autism at their 18- and 24-month well-child visits. Additional screening might be needed if a child is at high risk for ASD or developmental problems. Those at high risk include children who have a family member with ASD, have some ASD behaviours, have older parents, have certain genetic conditions, or who were born at a very low birth weight.

Parents' experiences and concerns are very important in the screening process for young children. Sometimes, the doctor will ask parents questions about the child's behaviours and combine those answers with information from ASD screening tools and his or her observations of the child. Read more about screening instruments on the Centers for Disease Control and Prevention (CDC) website.

Children who show developmental problems during this screening process will be referred for a second stage of evaluation.

Stage 2: Additional Evaluation

This second evaluation is with a team of doctors and other health professionals who are experienced in diagnosing ASD.

This team may include:

- *A developmental pediatrician—a doctor who has special training in child development*
- *A child psychologist and/or child psychiatrist—a doctor who has specialised training in brain development and behaviour*

- *A neuropsychologist—a doctor who focuses on evaluating, diagnosing, and treating neurological, medical, and neurodevelopmental disorders*
- *A speech-language pathologist—a health professional who has special training in communication difficulties*

The evaluation may assess:

- *Cognitive level or thinking skills*
- *Language abilities*
- *Age-appropriate skills needed to complete daily activities independently, such as eating, dressing, and toileting*

Because ASD is a complex disorder that sometimes occurs along with other illnesses or learning disorders, the comprehensive evaluation may include:

- Blood tests
- Hearing test

The outcome of the evaluation will result in a formal diagnosis and recommendations for treatment.

Diagnosis in older children and adolescents

ASD symptoms in older children and adolescents who attend school are often first recognised by parents and teachers and then evaluated by the school's special education team. The school's team may perform an initial evaluation and then recommend these children visit their primary health care doctor or doctors who specialise in ASD for additional testing.

Parents may talk with these specialists about their child's social difficulties, including problems with subtle communication. These subtle communication issues may include problems understanding tone of voice, facial expressions, or body language. Older children and adolescents may have trouble understanding figures of speech, humor, or sarcasm. Parents may also find that their child has trouble forming friendships with peers.

Diagnosis in adults

Diagnosing ASD in adults is often more difficult than diagnosing ASD in children. In adults, some ASD symptoms can overlap with symptoms of other mental-health disorders, such as anxiety or attention-deficit/hyperactivity disorder (ADHD).

Adults who notice the signs and symptoms of ASD should talk with a doctor and ask for a referral for an ASD evaluation. While testing for ASD in adults is still being refined, adults can be referred to a neuropsychologist, psychologist, or psychiatrist who has experience with ASD. The expert will ask about concerns, such as:

- *Social interaction and communication challenges*
- *Sensory issues*
- *Repetitive behaviours*
- *Restricted interests*

Information about the adult's developmental history will help in making an accurate diagnosis, so an ASD evaluation may include talking with parents or other family members.

Getting a correct diagnosis of ASD as an adult can help a person understand past difficulties, identify his or her strengths, and obtain the right kind of help. Studies are now under way to determine the types of services and supports that are most helpful for improving the functioning and community integration of transition-age youth and adults with ASD.

Changes to the diagnosis of ASD

In 2013, a revised version of the Diagnostic and Statistical Manual of Mental Disorders (DSM) *was released. This revision changed the way autism is classified and diagnosed. Using the previous version of the* DSM, *people could be diagnosed with one of several separate conditions:*

- *Autistic disorder*
- *Asperger's syndrome*

- *Pervasive developmental disorder not otherwise specified (PDD-NOS)*

In the current revised version of the DSM (the DSM-5), these separate conditions have been combined into one diagnosis called "autism spectrum disorder." Using the DSM-5, for example, people who were previously diagnosed as having Asperger's syndrome would now be diagnosed as having autism spectrum disorder. Although the "official" diagnosis of ASD has changed, there is nothing wrong with continuing to use terms such as Asperger's syndrome to describe oneself or to identify with a peer group.

The responses of the parent or guardian are indispensable in the course of the child's screening. If everything is ruled out, then there is no need to fear. In case some of these concerns are positive, the child will need to meet a specialist for proper examination and screening.

Further screening may involve ASD specialists like the occupational therapist, child psychologist, speech-language pathologist, neurologist and developmental pediatrician. These experts will verify the development of skills, such as language abilities, eating/nutrition, self-dressing and thinking capacity.

They make their judgment based on the standards of the Diagnostic and Statistical Manual of Mental Disorders (DSM-5) published by the American Psychiatric Association (APA), whose most recent edition (fifth edition) was released in 2013. Here, we notice that Asperger's syndrome falls as a band in the ASD. The DSM-5 takes into consideration five subtypes of the autism spectrum disorder. These include:

- *With or without accompanying intellectual impairment*
- *With or without accompanying language impairment*
- *Associated with a known medical or genetic condition or environmental factor*
- *Associated with another neurodevelopmental, mental, or behavioural disorder*

- *With catatonia (movement and behavioural abnormality arising from an unstable mental state).*

It is equally important for a genetic test to be carried out in order to eliminate conditions that could cause the above symptoms.

Causes of Autism and Asperger's syndrome

Causes of Autism

Here, we will look at the causes of these disease conditions. We have learnt that ASD is actually one disease with different degrees of severity or with different shades. Other documents will group the possible causes into genetic, environmental and physical. Here, we will look at them in a single block, as some of the causes conflict between environmental, physical or genetic. They include:

- **Having a close family member with autism**

Some experts explain that having an immediate family member suffering from any shade of autism spectrum disorder heightens the chances of the sibling or offspring suffering from the same condition. They claim that some genes that carry the traits of this condition may cross to fellow family members down the generation. In this case, only direct or indirect siblings of the sick or healthy carrier will inherit the genes and either express or simply carry them forward.

- **Genetic mutations**

There are a couple of factors that affect the mutation of genes in humans. They include exposure to radiation and carcinogenic chemicals, errors in DNA replication and instability of the purine or pyrimidine bases. Having undergone mutation, these genes may concern the coordination of the human behavioural pattern or the vocal aspect of the human body. This victim is, therefore, able to carry on the genetic deformity to his or her offspring, thus able to birth an autistic.

- **Fragile X syndrome and other genetic disorders**

Fragile X syndrome (FXS) is a congenital disease passed down from parents to their offspring that causes intellectual and developmental disabilities. It is equally called Martin-Bell syndrome. FXS is caused by a defect in a gene found on the X chromosome. A male human carries an X and a Y chromosome while a female carries two X chromosomes. These are called sex chromosomes. The defect of this gene prevents the proper making of the fragile X mental retardation 1 protein. This protein is said to play an important role in the proper functioning of the nervous system, though the proper functional mechanism of this protein is not well-established. A poor synthesis of this protein causes the symptoms characteristic of FXS.

- **Children born to older parents**

It is said that the quality of male and female gametes (sperm and ovum) depreciates with age. In this case, the gametes will not form a good underlying framework for a child to properly be formed; thus, the chances of birthing a child with a retarded mentality or low cognitive ability become heightened. It is equally possible that the physical state of a gestating (pregnant) mother can affect the aptitude of the developing fetus (even if the sperm or ovum or both are in good shape). In this second case, the aged mother may not be able to provide the nutrients required by the developing fetus to fully grow, considering that her metabolic efficiency has dropped considerably.

- **Low birth weight**

There are multiple factors that can lead to the birth of an underweight baby. These include multiple pregnancies, alcohol and drugs, smoking, malnutrition, stress, maternal disease or infection, cervical or uterine problems, malfunction of the placenta and fetal infection. An underweight child from any of these causes indicates that fetal development was not complete or inappropriate. If the brain happens to be one of them, coordination and other cognitive defects may possibly lead to autism.

- **Metabolic imbalances**

Metabolic imbalance is when the body cannot break down food or use food nutrients normally to build up required molecules and structures for one reason or another. In this case, we may have diabetes, hormonal imbalance or obesity. If the metabolism or structure in question has to do with those linked to coordination, an autistic offspring is a possibility.

- **Exposure to heavy metals and environmental toxins**

The presence of heavy metals or their poor processing is a possible cause of autism. A heavy metal like lead (Pb) is known to cause cognitive deficits, learning disabilities, behavioural delays, neurological immaturity and attention deficits; thus, it's a cause of ASD by definition.

- **A history of viral infections**

Research has shown that there are links between viral infections in a gestating mother and a surge in the possibility of bringing forth an autistic child. In this case, the viral infection may affect the nervous system or infect another part of the body, which triggers the malfunctioning of the nervous system.

- **Fetal exposure to medications such as valproic acid (Depakene) or thalidomide (Thalomid)**

Research has proven that the administration of valproate in the treatment of epilepsy and other neuropsychological disorders in pregnant mothers is a possible cause of ASD in newborns. Thalidomide sold under the brand name Thalomid is used for cancer cases and some host-versus-grafted tissue diseases. This drug is equally used to treat leprosy. Back in the 50s, this drug was used to treat pregnant women suffering from morning sickness. The latter not only caused ASD but a couple of deformities in children whose mothers took the drug.

Causes of Asperger's Syndrome

According to MillCreek, which treats causes and risk factors of Asperger's syndrome altogether, they elaborate that there is no single cause for the development of autism spectrum disorders, including Asperger's syndrome. However, when considering the complexity of the disorder and the fact that symptom severity varies, there are likely many different causes. Some current theories include:

Genetic: Research has determined that several genes appear to be involved in autism spectrum disorder. In some children, the presence of Asperger's syndrome can be associated with genetic disorders, such as Rett syndrome or Fragile X syndrome. Additionally, genetic changes may make a child more susceptible to autism spectrum disorder or create the possibility for environmental risks. Furthermore, other genes may affect brain development, how brain cells communicate or will determine the severity of symptoms.

Physical: Brain imaging studies have shown that there are structural and functional differences in specific areas of the brain in those who have Asperger's versus those who do not. These differences may be caused by the abnormal migration of the embryonic cells during fetal development, which then affects how the brain is wired and further goes on to affect the neural circuits that control thought and behaviour.

Environmental: Researchers are also exploring the impact that environmental factors, such as viral infections, prenatal complications, and air pollutants, may play in the development of autism spectrum disorders, like Asperger's syndrome.

Risk Factors:

- Being male
- Presence of a co-occurring mental health disorder, such as depression or anxiety
- Family history of autism spectrum disorders or other mental health conditions

- Being born 10+ weeks premature
- Having another medical condition, such as Fragile X syndrome, tuberous sclerosis, epilepsy, and Tourette syndrome
- Being born to older parents

Management of Kids with Autism and Asperger's syndrome

Considering there is no known cure for these conditions today, we use the word management to better express the way individuals with these conditions can be handled. The aim of this management is to help the individuals better interact socially or communicate accordingly. Another reason is for those who hurt themselves or close ones to stop being violent in the course of crisis. Therapies have been conceived in this light and appear as follows:

- **Communication and Behavioural therapies.** A couple of programs address the range of social, language and behavioural difficulties linked with ASD. Some of them focus on reducing violence or self-hurting, as well as teaching new skills. Others teach autistics how to better interact or communicate with each other. Applied behaviour analysis (ABA) can help autistics to learn new and better skills in order to handle multiple situations.

- **Educational therapies.** Most autistic children often respond positively when subjected to well-structured educational programs. The most ideal and impactful structures are made up of specialists who have a mastery of autistic disorders. They emphasise the improvement of social and communication skills. Behavioural patterns are checked, and education is adapted accordingly.

- **Home therapies.** Parents or guardians of autistic children can learn to play, communicate and interact with their children in ways that will enhance their socialization skills and behavioural patterns. Since the children live with their parents or guardians, this stands out as the most solicited therapy, considering that the children are made to adapt to their immediate environment in which they spend most of their existence.

- **Other therapies.** As mentioned earlier, there is a wide difference in the type of impairment when dealing with ASD. Therefore, autistics need different approaches, and psychologists are better placed to recommend the approach or therapy in handling any said behaviour.

- **Medications.** Keeping in mind that ASD has no cure, any medications administered in this case are meant to control the symptoms. Risperidone (Risperdal) has been found useful in treating irritability. Fluoxetine, paroxetine and sertraline have been used as antidepressants, though recent findings question their efficacy. It should be noted that some supplements can interact with medications and cause dangerous to lethal consequences.

Below is a detailed step-by-step approach to handling autistic children proposed by some therapists. This approach consists of three main methods, which are sub-listed into strategic points.

Method 1. Getting Help

1. **Seek Professional Assistance.** Health care providers rely on behavioural patterns and/or written questionnaires during routine checkups. There are equally screening tests that can be done during these visits. If your doctor does not regularly screen for autism, please request him/her to do so. It is true these patients are our loved ones and part of the family, but we can never do everything on our own. This is why it is always important to seek professional help. It will help them more than us struggling to manage things by ourselves.

2. **Understand that autistics differ from one another.** There is no one-sise-fits-all diagnosis for autism. Every individual needs a well-tailored management plan. The question, "What do autistics need?" should not be asked, but "What does this particular person need?" should remain key. Treat every child independent of any other. Do

not assume things, and do not attempt to treat a child in a particular way because autistic children are generally like this or like that. Work more on understanding your child and treat him following your notion of his temperament.

3. For example, an autistic person may possess excellent self-care skills and above-average school performance but require sensory integration therapy and social skills training. Another might instead be highly social but not able to care for his/herself and in need of counseling for depression.

4. **Consider Medications.** Though autism has no cure, as earlier mentioned, some of its challenging aspects and comorbid conditions can be helped through medication.

   - Anxiety
   - Elevated energy level
   - Self-injurious behaviour
   - Inability to concentrate
   - Depression
   - Seizures
   - Severe outburst of anger or aggression

5. Consult your health care provider to ensure your loved one is on the proper management plan with respect to their individual needs.

6. Consider comorbid conditions. Many autistic individuals also experience comorbid disabilities/health conditions, such as anxiety disorders, epilepsy, digestive problems, depression, attention deficit hyperactivity disorder (ADHD), oppositional defiant disorder (ODD), and more. These can all be treated.

Method 2. Choosing Therapies

1. **Try the Rapid Prompting Method (RPM) for developing communication skills, especially for nonverbal autistic individuals.** Rapid prompting involves continuously asking

questions to the autistic and letting him/her answer either in writing, pointing to a letter board, speaking, or whatever works best. This encourages the autistic person to communicate and relate more with the world.

2. **Consider Relationship Development Intervention (RDI) to teach social skills.** RDI emphasises developing skills, such as theory of mind, independent thinking, consideration of others, and more. It takes a long time for this therapy to be completed. This is because, as we already know, some, if not most of these autistic patients are slow and most often introverts. This means they will think about themselves and what they want before anything else. Some even go the extra mile of throwing tantrums whenever their wants are not given in time. This is just their nature, nothing of their making, so this therapy is aimed at changing their nature and perception of things, which is why it has to take a long time to go about it.

3. **Consider behavioural therapies such as Applied Behaviour Analysis (ABA) with caution.** Behavioural therapy can teach mechanical tasks using extrinsic rewards and can be useful for concrete skills, such as hand-washing, listening to the word "stop," and even tying shoes. Unfortunately, there are many negative stories of goals that involve compliance, forced normalization and abuse. Choose passionate therapists and make sure the focus is on teaching your loved one the skills they need and not forcing them to conform. Try as much as possible to follow recommendations when it comes to choosing a therapist so you don't fall into the hands of pseudo therapists.

4. **Try Cognitive Behavioural Therapy (CBT) to help with the anxiety and depression, which often accompany ASD.** CBT is a form of talk-on therapy that can help identify distorted or disoriented thoughts, such as "Everybody will laugh at me if I flap my hands" or "I am a burden to my family," and evaluate their accuracy.

5. **Try Sensory Integration Therapy (SIT) and a sensory diet to help with sensory issues.** A skilled therapist can work with you

and/or your loved one to provide strategies to meet the autistic person's needs.

- A sensory diet is a set of activities to do at home, like climbing trees, finger painting, swinging, blowing bubbles, and more. It can help meet the autistic person's needs and get them used to various stimuli. It can also be a lot of fun for them.

- The therapist can also help redirect harmful or poor habits (e.g., hitting one's head, scraping the hair, hitting the leg) towards ones that meet the same needs without necessarily causing harm (e.g., hitting a pillow, kicking a bag).

6. **Consider complementary and alternative treatments.** There exists no scientific evidence that any of them are helpful at all. Some involve specific risks, but some people find them useful. The following is a list of therapies that fit this category and examples of what they may involve:

- Energy therapy - reiki, Therapeutic Touch, acupuncture
- Homeopathy, alternative medical systems - aromatherapy
- Manipulative and body-based method - deep pressure, acupressure, hydro massage
- Mind-body intervention - auditory integration, meditation, dance therapy
- Biologically based therapy - using herbs, special diet, and vitamins
- Always consult a medical doctor before making any major change to your own or a loved one's diet or lifestyle. Some alternative therapies, such as chelation therapy, are potentially lethal. If the autistic person is upset by the therapy or fails to improve, a different therapy should be used.

7. **Watch for fake therapies and false claims.** From common snake oil peddlers to certified Board Certified Behaviour Analysts (BCBA), there are people who will distort truths and support ideas that can harm you or your loved one. Trust your instincts, don't let

fearmongering make you panic, and don't continue therapy if you think it is not working out for you or your loved one.

- Therapy should not be very painful or distressing. A therapist should take the patient's pain or unhappiness seriously. This is very important, as it can get to a point where the patient tends to dislike therapy, which becomes unmanageable. Some therapists might insist on getting particular results, pushing a little too hard and cause pain or and distress. This should be avoided.

- 40 hours of therapy per week is as intense as a full-time job. This can be extremely overwhelming. Younger persons do not have adult attention spans. Your child will be fine with just 1-2 hours per day, and there's no rush. You have got a lifetime with your patient, and you must be mindful that this patient cannot be cured, so all of this is just to manage the condition. So take your time and gain some patience. Always keep in mind that age matters, and if you meet a therapist who is not considering this, then quit, or else you could overwork a child or do less than required to an adult. Work accordingly and then watch closely how the patient evolves.

- Transparency is an indispensable request. Therapists should not prevent you from witnessing a situation or avoid your questions. Do as much as you can to be present during sessions. Do not let therapy work with your patient in your absence. When you follow the sessions, you tend to understand your patient more and know better how to manage day to day and, most importantly, in times of crisis.

- Take note that it's a warning sign should a therapist insist on working only with your patient and give excuses whenever you propose being present. This either means the therapist is not confident in what he or she is doing, meaning there might be a huge degree of unprofessionalism, or what he or she does is formal or not correct. So he either does not know the right thing to do or knows the right thing to do but not doing it.

- People or therapists who claim to cure autism are not being honest. As mentioned earlier, autism is more genetic, not caused by vaccines or parasites. Therefore, this means that such therapists do not have a mastery of what they claim they want to work on; they are charlatans, and you should flee from them. It is very important to avoid those who claim to cure autism, too, because they can end up giving you false hopes, making you think the condition will change with time. When time passes and change is not forthcoming, you start getting desperate and restless, which can greatly affect the patient.

- Your instincts matter much. If a therapist is telling you to ignore your feelings, that you're irrational, or that you would intervene if you see what is being done to your loved one, this is a problem. If you are a parent or caregiver to a patient, you create some sort of a bond after living together for some time. If your instincts tell you that something is not right with the therapy or therapist, take it seriously. Do not ignore it because this might just be what your patient needs to feel better and be understood better.

Method 3. Creating a Positive Environment

1. Treat your loved one and any other with kindness and respect. Autistic people can undergo huge amounts of pressure to perform "normally," and the best way to help them is to give them respect. Make it clear that you will need to listen to them. If they feel supported at home, they will communicate and adapt much better and feel happy. Also, the chances are that other people will treat your children the way they see you treat them. This means that if those around you see you giving a lot of attention to your children and being patient in understanding them and showing them respect, they, too, will try to do the same, making it easier for your autistic child to feel accepted. This kind of treatment makes it easier to manage the patient's condition.

2. Talk to your loved one often to encourage them to talk as well. Children learn to understand speech or language by hearing others speak. Talking to an uncommunicative person will help them to open up (even if the conversations are fairly one-sided in the beginning). If you know what their special interests or leisure are, start conversations about them.

- Read their body language and gesticulation as you talk to them. For example, if you ask your son, "Did you play with your friends today?" and he squeals happily and waves his arms, this is his answer, and it means he will like playing with them. This communication is a steppingstone and should be nurtured. Always remind yourself not to expect so much from your child so that you can appreciate the little he or she offers. With this knowledge, just squealing will be enough information to the parent and not necessarily a vocal phrase.

3. Presume competence. Act with the assumption that your loved one can hear and comprehend you, even if it doesn't look like it. Treat them like they are fundamentally good and intelligent or smart. Positive expectations can help them get happier. Remember, to them; life is all about appreciation and happiness. Also, constantly appreciate and compliment the little they do. This may encourage them to do more.

- If your loved one is in the room with you, assume they can hear what you're saying. If you complain about how difficult it is to live with an autistic child, they'll worry that they make your life worse by existing. Save your adult fears for when the child or children are out of the room. No normal child would like to be looked upon as a burden, and this is exactly what the child will think and feel upon stumbling over conversations like the aforementioned.

4. Be transparent about what's going on. Let them know the reality about themselves, that they're autistic. This can help them have words for their experiences and dismiss any confusion that they're "broken" or "bad." Let them know that they're just different, but that this is okay, and you love them the way they are. It is very important to make them know that they are loved just the way they are, so they don't start feeling a need to be like every other person, which cannot be attained since we know this situation is not reversible. When they are in this kind of position, it is very easy for a crisis to arise because they get stressed and desperate for a normal lifestyle. Also, being able to explain to some other person who they are keeps them conscious of themselves. Thus, an understanding of their personality is a step towards managing them.

Management of Adults with Autism and Asperger's syndrome

The management of ASD in adults is similar to children, the only difference being the age or late diagnosis. This means any abnormal behaviour or communication must have become part and parcel of the person's way of life, which will require much more effort to change it. At some point, it is easier to manage adults because they would have developed reasoning or adaptive skills to overcome the complications associated with this disorder, though it remains a major concern when these adaptive skills are detrimental. Therefore, we have a couple of therapeutic measures to this effect.

- **Cognitive behavioural therapy.** Having an autistic elderly person whose behavioural pattern has needs to be altered is not as easy as in a younger person. This, of course, is because the patient has become used to certain things that have gradually become a habit. As they say, old habits die hard, and it is also said that practice makes perfect. Thus, the patient has lived an entire life, practicing some habit, and the brain has become so used to it that instilling a change becomes more demanding than a child who's just started learning and been taught the right things from childhood. The therapist here needs an in-depth knowledge of the patient as well as a mastery of how to induce change in behaviour. For example, the autistic should be made to socialise and avoid repetitive gestures.

- **Speech therapy.** Since speech is mostly dependent on frequent vocal expression, it is best to keep communicating with the autistic for quite a long time while adapting with the possible changes that may take place. It is known that the emotional state affects speech. Therefore, the autistic should often be kept in the best of his emotions in the cause of this therapy. Keeping them in such a mood is very difficult but not impossible. It's difficult because their response to actions is not the same as many others, especially emotionally; therefore, within this time, caregivers and parents should try as much as possible to respect their routines and give them the kind of things they generally like as often as they want. This just might go a long way in facilitating the process.

- **Vocational therapy.** Studies have proven that most adult workers who are autistic are able to work successfully and full-time as well. In case any abnormalities show up in the course of this, a vocational therapist will be the best person to find solutions to maintain smooth job productivity. Vocational therapy is when work is being used as a therapy. The therapist makes sure to pick what the patient loves doing, without treating the patient as a patient but rather as an agent. By the end of the day, when the patient has been successful in doing the job, the satisfaction brings in a lot of positivity.

- **Medications.** Adult autistics require medications only when individual symptoms appear, such as anxiety or hyperactivity– medications like stimulants, antipsychotics and serotonin reuptake inhibitors (SSRIs).

Prevention of Autism and Asperger's syndrome

Prevention of Autism

ASD is an innate disease, and preventive measures are supposed to be taken exclusively on the parent's side to prevent an autistic offspring. In order to prevent this disorder, we have to make a throwback at the probable causes. Like they say, in order to kill a tree, dig out the roots.

i.   Parental screening and anamnesis

It is advisable that parents carry out thorough screening to make sure that they are not carrying genes that can result in the expression of faulty characteristics. This applies not just to the prevention of ASD but also for other congenital diseases like sickle cell anemia, heart conditions and diabetes type I. It is, therefore, advisable that people carrying similar genetic issues should not have a child together.

If genetic testing appears to be an issue, anamnesis or family history of possible autism spectrum disorder should be taken into consideration before conception and subsequent birth.

ii.   Timely diagnosis

Another way of preventing ASD is by carrying out early diagnosis and giving the autistic the adapted treatment and intervention to help sort any behavioural or emotional complications. The earlier it is done, the easier the management. This advice goes well for many other congenital diseases. Early screening is always very important because it helps the parents diagnose and control or, if possible, treat whatever illness is detected.

iii.   Shielding and non-administration of teratogens to gestating women.

If, for example, a radioactive source is shielded from the population, the chances of getting affected with the emissions get pretty much reduced. Similarly, non-administration of drugs, which can cause physical or functional defects in the human embryo or fetus (teratogens) to a pregnant woman, is a method of preventing possible autistic offspring. Equally, parents who do not smoke have greater chances of having healthy kids. Failure to drink alcohol during pregnancy is equally a plus. No matter how tempted a pregnant woman gets, it is always advisable to fight the temptation as much as possible. For a woman who is used to alcohol and has a hard time resisting it, those around her are encouraged to avoid drinking as much as possible because this can easily provoke the appetite for it. Sometimes, the husband, if he is the closest to her, is advised to accompany her in abstaining, which makes it easier for her. This is very important because alcohol can expose the baby more to ASD or other diseases, which can provoke the malformation of the fetus and/or the brain.

iv.   Mature birth

If parents have children at the required child-bearing age, it will greatly minimise the chances of having autistic children. This is because at the right child bearing age, the physiology of the parents is at its best for their kids. Pregnancy at an older age exposes the baby to ASD. After a survey was carried out amongst a cross-section of autistic children, it was realised that most of the parents were above 40 than below 30 years of age.

v.   Vaccination

Considering that some viral infections, such as rubella, are leading causes of ASD, pregestational vaccination can help prevent rubella-associated autism. If you can respect all vaccines during pregnancy, this might go a long way in helping not just autism but many other disorders.

vi.   Healthy living

Have regular medical check-ups, eat balanced meals, and exercising are basic preventive measures, not just for curable illnesses but indispensable for persons of child-bearing age. Making sure gestating mothers have good prenatal care and taking all recommended vitamins and supplements seals any possible loopholes. Due to cravings, some pregnant women end up eating particular things; however, they should be encouraged to fight these cravings and eat properly. The baby grows better when the mother leads a more responsible life. If possible, a family should change its entire eating habits when a pregnant woman is in the home. This is because most times, these women tend to want things they see or aromas they perceive. In this case, it might be a little easier for her to crave something she has access to than what she has not thought much of. The sight encourages the mind and provokes cravings, which might sometimes be unhealthy.

In this same light, the entire family is encouraged to embark on sporting activities every once in a while to encourage the pregnant woman. She might find it a little heavy or like a burden having to do this all by herself, but once the family makes her feel they are together in this, then she finds herself liking it.

Prevention of Asperger's syndrome

Just like autism, Asperger's syndrome can be prevented by the following measures as stated by NCBI.

1. Asperger's syndrome can be prevented by timely diagnosis and early intervention by the health experts. This is the best way to prevent behavioural and emotional complications related to this disorder.

2. Behavioural modification and parental counselling may also help. There are standard guidelines for medical management through psychiatric medication to control emotional/behavioural problems.

3. Also, mild stimulant medications that are provided to deal with restlessness, aggressiveness and attention deficit help people suffering from Asperger's Syndrome.

4. Medication is often combined with family and group therapy, and occupational therapeutic interventions to enhance daily living in society. Behavioural treatment is aimed at modifying parents' and teachers' responses towards a child's difficulties. Treatment is aimed at providing a structured environment to the children with scope for contingency management. How to prevent kids from being born with the above conditions as well as parents' exposure to predisposing factors.

Prevalence of Autism and Asperger's syndrome

Prevalence of Autism

Like most innate disorders, autism may not have well-established causes, but the prevalence has some factors which gives it high possibilities of occurrence. These include prevalence based on sex and that based on ethnicity.

Sex: According to the NCBI, the first published descriptions of autism has been a male-typical disorder: 8 of the 11 cases described by Kanner, and all 4 cases described by Asperger were male. Prevalence surveys conducted since have reported a range of male biases from 1.33:1 male: female (M:F) to 15.7:1, and a commonly referenced consensus ratio of ~4:1. Intelligence level affects this sex ratio: males are substantially over-represented among high-functioning cases, and males and females are more equally represented among cases with severe intellectual disability (ID). A 1999 review reported median sex ratios of 6:1 among normal-functioning subjects and 1.7:1 among cases with moderate to severe ID.

Several biological factors could explain this relationship between IQ and the sex ratio, but it should also be recognised that this could also, at least partially, reflect ascertainment bias. Co-morbid ID increases the females' likelihood of acquiring an ASD diagnosis, and conversely, high-functioning females may go undiagnosed. The wide variation in the sex ratio reported by different sites in the Autism and Developmental Disabilities Monitoring

(ADDM) Network and findings from large-scale population screening for ASD in a South Korean community where clinically ascertained samples show higher M:F ratios than less biased population screening are consistent with this hypothesis. Generally, high sex ratios have been found by studies that predominantly identified subjects via treatment facilities or disability registries, including more recent studies of records from Boston area hospital records and Taiwanese disability registries. In contrast, low sex ratios between 1.7:1 in high-functioning ASD cases and 2.3:1 in cases with ASD and co-morbid ID were found in an epidemiological, population-screening study for ASDs in Finland, although the same trend was not found in England, where a 9 to 1 M:F ratio was observed in high functioning individuals with an ASD. Overall, prevalence studies demonstrate that ASD is consistently over-represented in males compared to females. But currently, we do not understand the extent of this over-representation or the degree to which this male bias in prevalence is related to intellectual functioning or ascertainment methods in addition to the influence of sex-differential genetic or hormonal factors.

Ethinicty: According to the National Center for Biotechnology Information; *for 2 decades, autism prevalence has risen in the United States and now reaches 147 per 10,000 children diagnosed with autism spectrum disorders (ASDs) by 8 years of age and 21 per 10,000 children with autistic disorder (AD). The associated disabilities are characterised by atypical development of socialization and communication and the presence of restricted, repetitive interests and behaviours beginning in early childhood. Lower ASD prevalence in Hispanic and African American/black children (henceforth "black") than in non-Hispanic white children (henceforth "white") and variations in prevalence from 30 to 210 per 10,000 among Asians/Pacific Islanders (Asians/PIs) have been reported. Autism phenotype differences with regard to intellectual and language disabilities across race/ethnic groups in the United States may suggest differences in ASD etiology and disparities in diagnostic and treatment-related factors.*

The prenatal period is strongly implicated in ASD etiology; yet, except for parental age and some pregnancy complications, evidence is insufficient for many potential prenatal risk factors, including recently reported associations with immigration status of the mother. Epidemiology has a long tradition of using migration studies to understand how environmental and genetic factors contribute to disease risk in populations. The fact that 22% of children <6 years old born in the United States have immigrant parents opens a unique opportunity to consider the influence of nativity and race/ethnicity on the etiology of ASD.

We hypothesised that the prevalence of AD (Diagnostic and Statistical Manual of Mental Disorders, Revised Fourth Edition [DSM- IV-R]) and specific phenotypes, i.e., comorbid mental retardation (MR), expressive language, and emotional/behavioural deficits, differs by maternal race/ethnicity and nativity. We focused our investigation on children born and diagnosed in Los Angeles (LA) County, California, a highly diverse metropolitan region home to black (400,000 in 2010), Hispanic (4.7 million in 2009), and Asian/PI (1.4 million in 2012) residents with a high proportion of immigrants (30% in 2011) and 92 languages spoken by students of the LA Unified School District. Our findings have clinical implications for early identification and treatment of ASD and research implications that raise innovative hypotheses, not only for different racial/ethnic groups but specifically for large and diverse immigrant communities who vary in risk, protective factors, and access to health care.

According to the National Institute of Mental Health, they elaborate the following statistics in terms of prevalence:

The table below shows data from the most recent ADDM Network prevalence estimates (published March, 2020). Data were collected from health and special education records of 8-year-old children living in 11 areas of the United States during 2016.

- *Across the CDC surveillance sites, an average of 1 in every 54 (1.9%) 8-year-old children were identified as having ASD in 2016.*
- *ASD is 4.3 times more common in boys (3.0%) than in girls (0.7%).*

- *ASD is reported to occur in all racial and ethnic groups.*

Prevalence of Autism Spectrum Disorder in 8-year-olds (2016) Data Courtesy of CDC*				
		*Prevalence***	*Percent***	*About 1 in every "x" children***
Overall		*18.5 per 1,000*	*1.9%*	*1 in 54*
Sex	*Boys*	*29.7 per 1,000*	*3.0%*	*1 in 34*
	Girls	*6.9 per 1,000*	*0.7%*	*1 in 145*
Race/Ethnicity	*White*	*18.5 per 1,000*	*1.9%*	*1 in 54*
	Black	*18.3 per 1,000*	*1.8%*	*1 in 55*
	Asian/Pacific Islander	*17.9 per 1,000*	*1.8%*	*1 in 56*
	*Hispanic****	*15.4 per 1,000*	*1.5%*	*1 in 60*

*The percentage (i.e., rate per 100) was calculated by NIMH.
** Please see the measurement caveats regarding age below.
***All other groups are non-Hispanic.

Recent findings have given a reason why ASD is more prevalent in male than female children. In a research paper released on April 2nd 2020 via ScienceDaily, *A new study in Neuron offers clues to why autism spectrum disorder (ASD) is more common in boys than in girls. National Institutes of Health scientists found that a single amino acid change in the NLGN4 gene, which has been linked to autism symptoms, may drive this difference in some cases. The study was conducted at NIH's National Institute of Neurological Disorders and Stroke (NINDS).* (Neuroligin-4, X-linked is a protein that in humans is encoded by the NLGN4X gene. When it is linked on the Y chromosome, we talk of NLGN4Y).

Researchers led by Katherine Roche, Ph.D., a neuroscientist at NINDS, compared two NLGN4 genes, (one on the X chromosome and one on the Y chromosome), which are important for establishing and maintaining synapses, the communication points between neurons.

Every cell in our body contains two sex chromosomes. Females have two X chromosomes; males have one X and one Y chromosome. Until now, it was assumed that the NLGN4X and NLGN4Y genes, which encode proteins that are 97% identical, functioned equally well in neurons.

But using a variety of advanced technology, including biochemistry, molecular biology, and imaging tools, Dr. Roche and her colleagues discovered that the proteins encoded by these genes display different functions. The NLGN4Y protein is less able to move to the cell surface in brain cells and is, therefore, unable to assemble and maintain synapses, making it difficult for neurons to send signals to one another. When the researchers fixed the error in cells in a dish, they restored much of its correct function.

"We really need to look at NLGN4X and NLGN4Y more carefully," said Thien A. Nguyen, Ph.D., first author of the study and former graduate student in Dr. Roche's lab. "Mutations in NLGN4X can lead to widespread and potentially very severe effects in brain function, and the role of NLGNY is still unclear."

Dr. Roche's team found that the problems with NLGN4Y were due to a single amino acid. The researchers also discovered that the region surrounding that amino acid in NLGN4X is sensitive to mutations in the human population. There are a cluster of variants found in this region in people with ASD and intellectual disability, and these mutations result in a deficit in function for NLGN4X that is indistinguishable from NLGN4Y.

In females, when one of the NLGN4X genes has a mutation, the other one can often compensate. However, in males, diseases can occur when there is a mutation in NLGN4X because there is no compensation from NLGN4Y.

The current study suggests that if there is a mutation in NLGN4X, NLGN4Y is not able to take over because it is a functionally different protein. If the mutations occur in regions of NLGN4X that affect the protein levels, that may result in autism-related symptoms, including intellectual deficits. The inability of NLGN4Y to compensate for mutations in NLGN4X may help explain why males, who only have one X chromosome, tend to have a greater incidence of NLGN4X-associated ASD than females.

"The knowledge about these proteins will help doctors treating patients with mutations in NLGN4X better understand their symptoms," said Dr. Roche.

This work was supported and sponsored by the NIH Intramural Research Program.

Prevalence of Asperger's Syndrome

The prevalence of Asperger's syndrome does not really differ from autism. Therefore, like autism, there are more males affected with this disorder than females with quasi the same ratio. In terms of ethnicity, we observe a similar trend. This implies that the expression of any autistic disorder follows the same patterns as others on a global scale.

Perception of the public towards persons with Autism and Asperger's syndrome

According to the Edinburgh Research Archive, adults and children with autism are often subject to stigma. The present study sought to measure the public's attitude towards individuals with autism, particularly whether age, awareness of an individual's diagnosis, knowledge of autism and the participant's personal autistic traits affected emotional attitudes towards autistic individuals. We assessed the effect of exposure to autism on knowledge of the condition and evaluated the effects of the participants' emotional responses and knowledge of autism on the intention to volunteer with individuals with autistic spectrum disorder. Furthermore, we hoped to expand the limited literature available on studies of adults with autism, as the vast majority describe populations of autistic children. Participants were tested using an online questionnaire, which measured attitudes towards video clips of an adult and two children displaying autistic behaviours. Participants scored higher emotional attitudes towards adults rather than children. Sympathy ratings and desire to help differed in response to the age of the autistic individual. Furthermore, disclosing or concealing the diagnosis did not affect emotional attitudes. The participants' personal autistic traits affect their emotional responses towards the individual in the clip. Intent to volunteer was predicted by emotions and knowledge. However, while knowledge was enhanced by exposure to autism, it failed to predict the intent to volunteer. Adults and children with autism are perceived differently by the public, as behavioural expectations differ with age. Educating the public by altering their emotional response may be an effective tool for reducing the stigma associated with the developmental disorder.

In most third world countries, a severe state of autism spectrum disorder is regarded as some demonic possession or a curse inherited from the wrongdoings of the ancestors or the parents of the child. In some societies, this child is either banished or left to die in a secret place as a way to cleanse the effect of the presumed curse. If this child is not pulled through the latter, he is left to grow but will be despised by the community. In some communities in Cameroon and Nigeria, autistic children were not just the ones suffering from this ill-treatment, but twin births were also considered taboo and merited maltreatment or some sacrifice. But these barbaric acts have been completely eradicated thanks to human rights organisations, local sensitization and change of religious beliefs. Therefore, these societies are more open to talks not only in line with autism and Asperger's syndrome but other diseases and health conditions, which were formerly regarded to be linked with some superstition and weird religions. As it stands, most communities that tend to look at autistic patients as taboo or those possessed with some evil spirit are those whose patients suffer the most from it, of course. Just the reaction one puts forth upon seeing and interacting with an autistic goes a long way in soothing and making them feel accepted or making them feel rejected, thus worsening the condition. The perception of an autistic is the basis of managing this condition. Some autistic patients have gone as far as committing suicide just from how they were treated by those around them or those they come across from day to day. No matter the amount of therapy the patients get, how society reacts to them always counts a great deal in the management of autistic patients.

Comorbidity, Autism and Asperger's syndrome (Comorbidity and Autism Spectrum Disorder)

Studies have shown that individuals with Autism spectrum disorder, in most cases, have other disorders accompanying it. This is called comorbidity of ASD. Comorbidity is, therefore, the existence of two or more disorders in a particular individual. These comorbid conditions can appear at any time in the course of the child's development. Some may not show up until the child grows to an adolescent or even an adult. Sometimes, these conditions have symptoms and effects that greatly affect how well ASD therapies and interventions work. These disorders may be due to autism alone or as a result of another secondary disorder. It is, therefore, indispensable to identify these conditions and treat them separately or give an appropriately merged therapy and management procedure. These related disorders include:

1. Tuberous sclerosis

- Improper functioning of the kidney
- Difficulties in breathing
- Hydrocephalus; accumulation of fluid in the brain

These problems can either be mild to severe, and it is possible to have only a few of these problems as well as a wide range. Members of the same family may be affected in varied ways by tuberous sclerosis.

Tuberous sclerosis is known to be caused by mutations in either the Tuberous Sclerosis Complex (TSC1) or TSC2 gene. These genes are involved in the regulation of cell growth, and the mutations lead to uncontrolled growth as well as multiple tumours throughout the body. In around three in every four cases, this genetic disorder occurs for no apparent reason in people without any affected family members. In the remaining one in four cases, the disorder is passed on to an offspring by its parents. Only one carrier-parent of this faulty gene is needed to pass it on, and a parent who has one of the faulty genes has a one in two chance of passing it down to each child they have. In this case, the parent may be a carrier of the faulty gene and have tuberous sclerosis, although it may be pretty mild, and they do not realise.

Like autism itself, there is no cure for tuberous sclerosis, but there is a range of treatments for many of the issues caused by the disorder.

For example:

- Epilepsy may be controlled with medication or even surgery in some cases
- Out of classroom educational support can help children with learning disabilities
- Poor behavioural skills and psychiatric problems, like anxiety or depression, can be treated with behavioural interventions and medication
- Brain tumours can be removed surgically or shrunk with medication
- Facial rashes can be treated with laser therapy or medication applied in the skin
- Medication can either help control symptoms caused by reduced kidney function or help shrink kidney tumours
- Pulmonary problems can be treated medically

Tests to prove organ functionality in people with tuberous sclerosis will be helpful to detect affected organs.

2. Neurofibromatosis

Neurofibromatosis type is a genetic condition that causes tumours to grow along the nerves. The tumours are usually benign but may cause a range of symptoms. According to the level of severity and frequency of occurrence, neurofibromatosis is divided into two types: 1 and 2, abbreviated NF1 and NF2, respectively, with NF2 much less common than NF1. These are treated separately, as they have different symptoms and causes. Though, in this context, they coexist with autism.

Neurofibromatosis type 1

Like autism, NF1 is an inborn condition, although some symptoms develop gradually over many years. The severity of the condition can vary considerably from one person to another. In most cases, the skin is affected, leading to symptoms such as:

- Pale, coffee-coloured patches
- Soft, benign tumours on or under the skin
- Clusters of freckles in unusual places – like the armpits, groin and under the breast

Some health problems are often associated with NF1, such as learning difficulties. Less commonly, NF1 is associated with a rare type of cancer known as malignant peripheral nerve sheath tumours. Similar to autism, NF1 is caused by a faulty gene. If the NF1 gene is faulty, it leads to uncontrolled growth or tumours developing in the nervous system. In half of all cases of NF1, the faulty gene is passed from a parent to their offspring. Only one parent needs to have the faulty gene for their child to run a risk of developing the condition. If the mother or father has the faulty gene, there's a one in two chance that each child they bear will develop NF1. In other cases, the faulty gene appears to be expressed spontaneously. It's unclear why this happens. If a child develops NF1 spontaneously, it is highly unlikely any further children you have will also develop the condition. However, a person who develops NF1 spontaneously can pass the condition to their children. It is usually easy to diagnose NF1 in autistic adults and older children by checking for the typical symptoms. NF may be diagnosed in babies who show symptoms of NF1 from birth. However, it is not always possible to make a firm diagnosis in early childhood because some symptoms take years to develop. If NF1 is suspected, further tests, such as echography, blood tests or a biopsy, may be recommended. This is to assess whether the child has other symptoms or conditions associated with NF1. If there is uncertainty about the diagnosis, the child should be able to have a blood test to see whether he has the faulty NF1 gene. However, this blood test is not totally reliable: around 5% of children who test negative for the faulty gene still develop NF1. Thus, it is advisable that couples with a family history of NF1 may need to consider their options before having a baby. The general practitioner can refer you to a genetic counsellor to discuss your options.

These may include:

- Having a child with a donor ovum or sperm
- Adopting a child
- Having either a chorionic villus sampling or amniocentesis test during pregnancy to see if the baby will have NF1

There's currently no cure for NF1 as the case with autism, but treatment involves regular monitoring and managing any problems as they occur.

Treatment can involve:

- Surgical procedures to remove tumours and improve bone abnormalities
- Medication to control secondary conditions, such as high blood pressure
- Physiotherapy
- Psychological support
- Pain management

Careful monitoring and treatment can help people with NF1 and autism live a full life. However, there's a risk of developing serious problems, such as certain types of cancer, that can reduce life expectancy.

Neurofibromatosis type 2

Just like NF1, NF2 is covered separately because it has different symptoms and causes. Almost everyone with NF2 develops tumours along the vestibulocochlear nerves (nerves responsible for hearing and balance). These usually cause symptoms such as:

- Hearing loss, which gradually gets worse over time
- Hearing of ringing or buzzing in the ears (tinnitus)
- Imbalance, particularly when moving in the dark or walking on uneven ground

Other tumours can grow inside the brain or spinal cord or along the nerves to the arms and legs. This can lead to weakness in the arms and legs and migraine or persistent headaches. Neurofibromatosis type 2 (NF2) is equally caused by a faulty gene. If the NF2 gene is faulty, it leads to uncontrolled growths developing in the nervous system. In half of all the cases with NF2, the faulty gene is passed from a parent to their child. Just like NF1, only one parent needs to have the faulty gene for their child to be at risk of developing the condition. If either the mother or father has the faulty gene, there is half a chance that each child they have will develop NF2. In other cases, the faulty gene appears to develop spontaneously. It's unclear why this happens.

If an autistic child develops NF2 spontaneously, it is highly unlikely any further children the parent has will also develop the condition. However, a person who develops NF2 spontaneously can pass the condition to their children. About one in three autistics with NF2 have a form of the disease called mosaic NF2. The symptoms of mosaic NF2 are milder and often restricted to a certain area or side of the body. People with mosaic NF2 have a lower than the usual half chance risk of having a child with NF2. It's usually easy to diagnose NF2 in adults and older autistic children by checking for the typical symptoms. It may be diagnosed in babies who express symptoms of NF2 from birth. However, it is not always possible to make a firm diagnosis before a child is 5 years old because some symptoms take years to develop. If NF2 is suspected, further tests – such as scans, hearing tests, sight tests or blood tests –

may be recommended, just like with NF1. This is to assess whether the child has other symptoms or conditions associated with NF2. If there's uncertainty about the diagnosis, the child may be able to have a blood test to see whether they have the faulty NF2 gene. However, the test is not completely reliable and may not find an issue in the NF2 gene in all people with NF2 symptoms. There's presently no cure for NF2. Treatment involves regular monitoring and treating any problems as they occur. Surgery can be used to remove most tumours, although there is a high risk of causing problems, such as complete deafness or facial weakness. Therefore, the risks and potential benefits need to be carefully considered before treatment. Most autistics with NF2 eventually develop significant hearing loss, and hearing aid or lip reading remain their solutions of choice. Special implants can sometimes be inserted to improve a person's hearing ability.

NF2 is likely to get worse over time, although the speed at which this happens varies considerably. However, most people with NF2 eventually lose their hearing totally, and some people require a wheelchair or other type of mobility device. Tumours that develop inside the brain and spinal cord can place strain on the body and shorten life expectancy. The symptoms of neurofibromatosis type 2 (NF2) typically start developing during the late teens or early twenties, but they may develop at any age. The hearing problems caused by this condition are similar to those of NF1. Less common symptoms include vertigo – when one has the feeling of spinning or everything around you is spinning – nausea and vomiting. Due to the continuous growth of the tumours over time, there are eventually additional symptoms such as:

- Numbness in parts of the face
- Weakness of the tongue – this can cause slurred or unusual-sounding speech and difficulty swallowing (dysphagia)
- Pain on the face – although this is not common

About two in three people with NF2 develop cloudy patches in the lens of the eye (cataracts).

Cataracts can make an autistic's vision blurred or misty. However, they're usually mild in NF2 and rarely cause serious vision complications. Cataracts are normally associated with old age, but they can develop in autistic children and young adults with NF2. It is also known that tumours can develop under the skin and grow to around the sise of a golf ball and can be very painful if they develop along a section of nerves. Some people with NF2 may also develop a relatively small number of coffee-coloured patches on their skin, called café au lait spots. But having lots of these spots is more of an NF1 than NF 2 type of neurofibromatosis. Many people with NF2 will develop a complication called peripheral neuropathy. This can cause a wide range of symptoms, including:

- A feeling of pins and needles in the affected body part
- Numbness and a reduced ability to feel pain or temperature changes – particularly in the feet
- A burning sensation – usually in the feet and legs, followed by the hands and arms as the neuropathy progresses
- Muscle weakness

Around half the number of autistics with NF2 develop one or more benign tumours inside their brain. These are called meningiomas. Meningiomas may cause no noticeable problems. However, they can sometimes lead to an increase in pressure in and around the brain, causing symptoms such as:

- Severe headaches
- Vomiting
- Seizures (fits)
- Vision disturbances – like double vision

The tumours can also disrupt certain brain functions. Depending on where they are, they may cause:

- Personality changes
- Weakness or numbness in one side of the body

- Difficulty speaking, understanding words, writing and reading (aphasia)
- Vision problems
- Fits or blackouts
- Memory problems
- Loss of smell (anosmia) or a sensation of strange smells (phantosmia)
- Unsteadiness, loss of co-ordination and difficulty walking
- Difficulty speaking and swallowing

Around one in two autistics with NF2 develop one or more benign tumours inside their spinal cord. These are called ependymomas. Of those who develop ependymomas, about one in two won't have any noticeable symptoms. But those who do may experience:

- Back pain
- Muscle weakness
- Unpleasant physical sensations in some parts of the body – such as numbness, tingling, or a "crawling" sensation on the skin

Treatment for neurofibromatosis type 2 (NF2) involves regular monitoring. Any problems are treated by a team of health professionals. Every autistic with NF2 requires regular monitoring to check for signs of any problems developing and to arrange treatment if necessary.

Monitoring NF2 usually involves:

- An annual MRI scan to check whether any new tumours have developed and whether any existing tumours have grown larger
- An annual eye test to check for cloudy patches at the front of the eye (cataracts)
- An annual hearing test to check the extent of any hearing loss

Depending on the symptoms, more frequent tests may sometimes be required.

It is advisable to contact a specialist if any new symptoms develop between examinations or if existing symptoms get worse. The development of tumours is one of the main problems associated with NF2. The best treatment is not always obvious. Many tumours are small and may not grow large enough to cause any complications, but others can be large and significantly affect wellbeing and life itself. It's possible to surgically remove some large tumours, but the risks can often outweigh the benefits. For example, removing tumours from the nerve tissue next to the ears could further damage hearing and cause paralysis of the facial muscles. Removing tumours from the spinal cord carries a small risk of damaging the spinal cord, which could also cause some degree of paralysis. However, in some cases, surgery may be required to prevent potentially serious complications, such as a tumour growing so large and risking brain damage. For smaller tumours, a type of radiotherapy known as the "gamma knife" may be an option. No actual knife is involved – rather, a tightly focused beam of gamma radiation is used to shrink a tumour. Compared to surgery, this treatment carries some risks. There's a possibility the gamma radiation could result in new tumours becoming cancerous. The chances of this are thought to be quite small, but it needs to be considered when weighing up the treatment options. For autistic persons with NF2, it is likely that hearing will get worse over time, so he may benefit from a hearing aid or learning to lip read. One option may be a surgically implanted electrical device called a hearing implant. There are two types of hearing implant used in NF2:

- Cochlear implants
- Auditory brainstem implants (ABIs)

Cochlear implants and ABIs have an external microphone, which receives and processes sounds. These signals are relayed into an internal receiver before being carried through wires to electrodes, either in the cochlea (the coiled, spiral tube inside the inner ear) or the brainstem itself. If a patient needs an ABI fitted, the surgeon will have to first remove any tumours from the hearing nerves. It should be known that the implants restore only some degree of hearing but can make lip reading much easier. As with all other types of surgery, there's a risk of complications. Some can be serious, like the infection of the outer layer of the brain (meningitis). These risks need to be considered when deciding the best way to manage the hearing problems. Another optional skill is learning to lip read. The treatment centre should be able to recommend a hearing therapist or another healthcare professional qualified to teach lip reading.

Hypothyroidism

The thyroid gland is a small butterfly-shaped gland in the neck, just in front of the windpipe or trachea. One of its principal functions is to produce hormones that help regulate the body's metabolism (the process that turns food into energy). These hormones are triiodothyronine (T3) and thyroxine (T4). Many of the body's functions slow down when the thyroid does not produce enough of these hormones, a condition we call hypothyroidism. Like other associated disorders in an autistic, hypothyroidism equally occurs. Common signs of hypothyroidism are tiredness, weight gain and depression. If any of these symptoms persist, it is advisable to see a general practitioner and ask to be tested for an underactive thyroid. An underactive thyroid can often be successfully treated by taking daily thyroid hormone tablets to provide the hormones the thyroid would have been producing. There is no way of preventing low thyroid functioning. Most cases are caused either by the immune system attacking the thyroid gland and damaging it (autoimmunity) or by damage to the thyroid that occurs during some treatments for a hyperactive thyroid or thyroid cancer. Apart from autism, a condition called Hashimoto's disease is the most common type of autoimmune reaction that causes an underactive thyroid. It is not clear what causes Hashimoto's disease, but it runs in family genes. It's also common in people with another immune system disorder, such as type 1 diabetes and vitiligo. Symptoms of underactive thyroid are often similar to those in other conditions, and they usually develop slowly, so one may not notice them for years. The only accurate way of finding out whether an autistic has a thyroid problem is to have a thyroid function test, where a blood sample is tested to measure the hormonal levels. Studies have shown that though hypothyroidism can affect both male and female autistic persons, it is more common in females. While some autistic persons develop this complication later in life, others are born with it. Treatment for an underactive thyroid involves taking daily hormone replacement tablets, called levothyroxine, to raise thyroxine levels. The patient will initially have regular blood tests until the correct dose of levothyroxine is reached. This can take quite a while to get right. Once the patient reaches the correct dose, he/she will usually have a blood test once a year to monitor the hormone levels, though treatment remains a must for the rest of the patient's life. However, a proper treatment plan will ensure a normal and healthy way of life. In autistic persons, if an underactive thyroid isn't treated, it can lead to complications, including heart disease, goitre, pregnancy problems and a life-threatening condition called myxoedema coma (although the latter is very rare). Many symptoms of an underactive thyroid (hypothyroidism) are the same as those of other conditions, so it can easily be confused for something else. Elderly autistic persons suffering from hypothyroidism may develop memory problems and depression. Children may experience slower growth and development. Teenagers may start puberty earlier than normal. Later symptoms of an underactive thyroid include:

- a low-pitched and hoarse voice
- a puffy-looking face
- thinned or partly missing eyebrows
- a slow heart rate
- hearing loss
- anemia

Worldwide, a lack of dietary iodine is a common cause of an underactive thyroid because the body needs iodine to make thyroxine. Babies are sometimes born with an underactive thyroid without necessarily being autistic. In this case, the thyroid gland does not develop properly in the womb. This is called congenital hypothyroidism and is uncommon. It's usually picked up during routine screening soon after birth. A problem with the pituitary gland can also lead to an underactive thyroid. The pituitary gland is located at the base of the brain and regulates the thyroid. Therefore, damage to the pituitary gland is likely to lead to an underactive thyroid. It should equally be noted that an underactive thyroid has also been linked to some viral infections or some medicines used to treat other conditions, such as:

- Lithium – a medicine sometimes used to treat some mental health conditions, including depression and bipolar disorder
- Amiodarone – a medicine sometimes used to treat arrhythmia (irregular heartbeats)
- Interferons – a class of medicine used to treat certain types of cancer and hepatitis C

It's very important that an underactive thyroid (hypothyroidism) is diagnosed as soon as possible.

1. Congenital deafness

Congenital deafness is a situation where a child is born with the inability to hear due to genetic causes or other influential factors, which might have affected the fetus in the mother's uterus. According to research from the National Center for Biotechnology Information, *a group of 199 children and adolescents (153 boys, 46 girls) with autistic disorder was audiologically evaluated. Mild to moderate hearing loss was diagnosed in 7.9% and unilateral hearing loss in 1.6% of those who could be tested appropriately. Pronounced to profound bilateral hearing loss or deafness was diagnosed in 3.5% of all cases, representing a prevalence considerably above that in the general population and comparable to the prevalence found in populations with mental retardation. Hearing deficits in autism occurred at similar rates at all levels of intellectual functioning, so it does not appear that the covariation with intellectual impairment per se can account for all of the variance of hearing deficit in autism. Hyperacusis was common, affecting 18.0% of the autism group and 0% in an age-matched non-autism comparison group. In addition, the rate of serous otitis media (23.5%) and related conductive hearing loss (18.3%)*

appeared to be increased in autistic disorder. The study emphasises the need for auditory evaluation of individuals with autism in order to refer those with pronounced to profound hearing loss for aural habilitation and to follow those with mild to moderate hearing loss because of the risk of deterioration.

Treating autistic children with this condition requires an application of adaptive skills. Sign language is one of the basic forms of training these cases. Though, at one point, it looks like a mathematical equation with many unknowns due to the difficulties involved in managing autism on its own less the lack of auditory senses. Some auditory devices and implants can equally be used to enhance hearing in these patients. Like every other condition and disorder, it is always advisable to diagnose hearing sensitivity in autistic children early enough so that curative measures can be taken on time.

2. Congenital visual impairment

This is a child's inability to see due to a malformation in the course of gestation. The child is thus born blind and, in this case, with links to an autistic disorder. The World Health Organisation (WHO) defines visual impairment as vision of less than 3/60, that is unable to see at 3 m what someone with typical vision can see at 60 m within a less than 5° field. In as much as it is a congenital disorder, visual impairment can equally be due to other associating disorders with autism, especially when the optic nerves get affected by a tumour or any other deformity. According to Springer post; *seven studies explored the incidence of visual impairments in people with ASD and found a higher incidence of strabismus (squint) (8.3%) than in a comparable child population (1.5 to 5.3%). Eleven studies identified behavioural traits common to both autistic and visually impaired populations.*

Depending on the extent to which this impairment occurs, the ophthalmologist can place the patient under corrective treatment as well as advise for corresponding education.

3. Epilepsy

Epilepsy is a neurological disorder marked by sudden recurrent episodes of sensory disturbance, loss of consciousness, or convulsions, associated with abnormal electrical brain activity. This can occur due to nervous obstruction at the level of the brain as a result of tumours, like in the case with Neurofibromatosis. These tumours gradually expand and obstruct the normal flow of nerve impulses.

First of all, the medical doctor will need to find out if the patient had a seizure. Next, it is important to find out what type of seizure or epilepsy syndrome best explains what happened. Doing this usually requires a couple of steps:

- A detailed medical history
- Blood tests
- Electroencephalogram (EEG) tests
- Brain imaging tests, like computed tomography (CT) and magnetic resonance imaging (MRI) scans

The timing of each step may differ since each person is different.

EEG tests and brain imaging tests give information about the electrical activity in the patient's brain, what his/her brain looks like, and what might be causing the seizures. Sometimes, the medical practitioner might order a test more than once to make sure it is accurate.

The doctor will consider all this information, including how the patient is feeling and how the seizures may be affecting his/her brain, to make a diagnosis. If the doctor gets new information later, she might change the initial (first) diagnosis.

It is important for the patient to keep in touch with the health care team. If new symptoms start showing up, or if the seizures are not responding to treatment, it might be time to take another look at the diagnosis.

If the medics think that the seizures are not ameliorating, they will probably refer the patient to a neurologist. A neurologist is a medical practitioner with special training in disorders of the brain, including epilepsy, though some neurologists have special training in epilepsy and spend most of their time treating people with epilepsy. They are called epileptologists.

In other cases, this condition can be treated by surgically removing the tumours after analyzing the risk/benefit status of the procedure. In other cases, anti-epileptic drugs are administered. Generally, autistic individuals with epilepsy have a relatively short life span.

4. Neuromuscular disorders

Neuromuscular disorders affect the muscles and their direct nervous system control. This can be due to problems with the central nervous control, which can lead to spasticity or some degree of paralysis from both lower and upper motor neuron disorders, depending on the condition and nature of the problem.

As far as the condition is concerned, neuromuscular disorders are diagnosed using a range of tests, including electrical tests known as nerve conduction studies (to measure the ability of nerves to conduct electricity), electromyography (EMG) to examine the health of the muscle, blood tests, muscle biopsies and genetic testing.

Neuromuscular Disorders present a multi-disciplinary approach to the management and therapeutic treatment of the full range of neuromuscular disorders and resulting complications – which becomes a serious concern in autistic persons. Some common drug-based interventions include the administration of immunosuppressive drugs that can treat certain muscle and nerve diseases as well as diseases of the nerve-muscle junctions.

5. Connective tissue disorders affecting muscle function

Connective tissue disorders refer to a group of disorders involving the protein-rich tissue that supports organs and other parts of the body. Mixed connective tissue disease is a term used by some medical specialists to describe a disorder characterised by features of systemic lupus erythematosus, systemic sclerosis, and polymyositis. Raynaud syndrome, joint pain, various skin abnormalities, muscle weakness, and problems with internal organs can equally develop. Examples of connective tissue are fat, bone, and cartilage. There are more than 200 disorders that can affect the connective tissue, and the presence of autism highlights the possibility of most.

A common symptom of connective tissue disease is nonspecific fatigue. Depending on which connective tissue disease is present and how active it is, a wide variety of symptoms are likely to occur. These include fevers, muscle and joint pain and stiffness, weakness, and a couple more symptoms. Blood tests are done to determine the levels of antinuclear antibodies (ANA) and an antibody to ribonucleoprotein (RNP), which are present in most people who have mixed connective tissue disease. Specialists who can be involved in the care for these patients include neurologists, cardiologists, pulmonologists, and nephrologists, though specialists with a particular interest in mixed connective tissue disease are rheumatologists.

Some medications commonly used in the treatment of autoimmune connective tissue diseases include corticosteroids. These medications help prevent the immune system from attacking your cells and prevent inflammation.

6. Hereditary disorders affecting glucocorticoid levels

Hereditary glucocorticoid disorder is a condition that occurs when the adrenal glands, which are hormone-producing glands located on top of each kidney, do not produce certain glucocorticoid hormones or produce a surplus – though cases of hypo glucocorticoid weigh out. These hormones, which include cortisol and corticosterone, help the immune system function, play a role in maintaining normal blood sugar levels, help trigger nerve cell signaling in the brain and serve many other purposes in the body. This disorder can be transmitted along the family line, which makes it hereditary.

A shortage of adrenal hormones (adrenal insufficiency) leads to the signs and symptoms of hereditary glucocorticoid deficiency. These signs and symptoms often show up in infancy or early childhood. Most affected children first develop hypoglycemia (low blood sugar). These hypoglycemic children can fail to grow or fail to gain weight at the expected rate (failure to thrive). If left untreated, hypoglycemia can lead to seizures (due to poor glucose to the brain), learning difficulties, and other neurological problems. Hypoglycemia that is left untreated for prolonged periods can lead to neurological damage and subsequent death. Other features of hereditary glucocorticoid disorders can include recurrent infections and skin coloring darker than other family members (hyperpigmentation).

7. **There are many types of hereditary glucocorticoid disorders, which are distinguished by their genetic cause.**

As far as treatment is concerned, genetic counseling is a possibility. Another form of treatment consists of replacement therapy with oral hydrocortisone in case of deficiencies. A dosage of 10-12 mg/m2/day (usually divided into three doses) normalises cortisol and reduces, but rarely normalises, adrenocorticotropic hormone (ACTH).

8. Fragile X syndrome

Fragile X syndrome (FXS), a genetic disorder characterised by mild-to-moderate intellectual disability, remains a comorbid condition in autistic persons. It should be recalled that this disorder has been discussed earlier in this book.

9. Sotos syndrome

Sotos syndrome is an autistic associable disorder characterised by a distinctive facial appearance, overgrowth in childhood, and learning disabilities or delayed development of mental and movement abilities. Characteristic facial features include a long, narrow face; a high forehead; flushed or reddened cheeks; and a small, pointed chin. Most persons with Sotos syndrome show signs of autism, according to the largest-yet study of people with the rare genetic condition. Sotos syndrome has been known to affect about 1 in 14,000 people.

There is no standard line of treatment for Sotos syndrome, and treatment depends on the symptoms portrayed. Sotos syndrome is not a life-threatening disorder, and patients may have a normal life expectancy unless other autistic associable disorders are involved. The initial abnormalities of Sotos syndrome usually resolve as the growth rate becomes normal after the first few years of an individual's life.

10. A variety of chromosomal disorders

Many cases of autism are reportedly caused by several abnormal genes acting in harmony. Studies on chromosomal aberrations in autism to find potential gene markers for the neuropsychiatric disorder show that most of the chromosomal disorders are implicated in the genesis of autism. However, aberrations on the long arm of Chromosome 15 and numerical and structural abnormalities of the sex chromosomes have been most frequently registered. These chromosomes appear to hold particular potential in the search for candidate genes responsible for any said disorder.

Some Famous people with ASD

With respect to information published on Remedy Health Media and other sites, we read the following:

Dan Aykroyd

Comedian actor Dan Aykroyd was expelled from two schools as a child and was later diagnosed with Asperger's Syndrome, a high functioning form of autism now considered part of the autism spectrum disorder diagnosis in the 1980s. In an interview with the Daily Mail, Aykroyd shared that one of his symptoms of ASD was his obsession with ghosts and law enforcement. Aykroyd goes on to credit this symptom of ASD as a catalyst for Ghostbusters. "My very mild Asperger's has helped me creatively," says comedic star Dan Aykroyd. "I sometimes hear a voice and think: 'That could be a character I could do.'"

Susan Boyle

Britain's Got Talent singing sensation Susan Boyle was diagnosed with Asperger's Syndrome as an adult. The Scottish singer, who was misdiagnosed with brain damage at birth, told The Guardian that her diagnosis helps her have a better understanding of herself. Bullied as a child because she was "different," Boyle went on to become a bestselling artist who also had a cameo role in the film, The Christmas Candle. Though Boyle also struggles with depression and mood swings, she now knows how to cope with and manage her symptoms, and credits having a great team of supportive people with helping her thrive.

Albert Einstein

Okay, we don't know for sure. But, according to autism expert Simon Baron-Cohen from Cambridge University, Einstein showed many signs of Asperger's syndrome. Other experts agree, including Michael Fitzgerald, professor of psychiatry at Trinity College in Dublin. He's also added to the list: Isaac Newton, George Orwell, H. G. Wells Ludwig Wittgenstein, Beethoven, Mozart, and Hans Christian Andersen.

Temple Grandin

Temple Grandin, a professor of Animal Science at Colorado State University and author of several books, including Thinking In Pictures and The Way I See It, didn't begin speaking until she was almost four years old. Like Daryl Hannah, when Grandin was diagnosed with autism as a child, institutionalization was the recommended treatment. Her parents disagreed. In addition to her writing, Grandin is a prominent speaker on both autism and animal behaviour. Temple Grandin's work has reshaped the way livestock are handled, thanks in a large part to her unique insight into how an animal's mind works. But today, she's best known for giving the world a unique insight into how the autistic mind works. Her books have helped tear down the stigma around autism and helped others to better understand how people with autism see the world.

Daryl Hannah

Actress Daryl Hannah was diagnosed with autism as a child. In an interview with People Magazine, Hannah opened up about her "debilitating shyness" as a child and fear of fame as an adult. Hannah shared with People Magazine that she was diagnosed at a time when autism was largely misunderstood, and her doctors recommended medication and institutionalization. Though her mother refused this treatment, she remained socially isolated and found solace in movies. This inspired her focus on acting. The Splash and Kill Bill actress has been fairly public with her childhood diagnosis of Asperger's. It is perhaps because of this that Hannah mostly stays clear of Hollywood anymore.

Sir Anthony Hopkins

Oscar award-winning actor Sir Anthony Hopkins was also diagnosed with Asperger's Syndrome, though when he was diagnosed remains unclear. Hopkins references learning differences as a child in media interviews as well as obsessive thinking and difficulty maintaining friendships even as an adult. Hopkins does credit ASD with his unique ability to look at people differently and deconstruct a character.

Heather Kuzmich

America's Next Top Model contestant, Heather Kuzmich, gave viewers a behind the scenes look at Asperger's Syndrome during the 2007 season of the show. Living in a house with twelve strangers/competitors presented challenges for Kuzmich as she dealt with jokes she didn't quite understand, decoding difficult social innuendo, and working through other symptoms (such as difficulty holding eye contact) as the show progressed. Kuzmich was voted viewer favorite eight weeks in a row during the competition and ended up in the top five.

While these ASD success stories represent a small sample of what ASD people can do, they do provide inspiration for the many kids out there learning to work through their own symptoms and find their passion. When young people have others to look up to, they learn that they can carve out their own paths at their own pace to leave their marks on the world as well.

According to research from other trusted sites, they reveal the following:

Courtney Love

Courtney Love, singer of Hole, was diagnosed as "mildly autistic" when she was a young girl. Though she was unusually intelligent, she struggled with school and social interactions.

Alonzo Clemons

Alonzo Clemons's IQ is somewhere between 40 and 50 — but somehow, he is capable of creating incredibly detailed and lifelike 3D sculptures of animals. "No one taught him to do this," says Nancy Mason, his assistant. For Clemons, she says, sculpting is an unstoppable instinct. "When they took away his clay, he would sculpt anything he could get his hands on."

Matt Savage

Composer and pianist Matt Savage taught himself how to read music when he was just six-years-old. By the time he was 11, his music career was so successful that he was signed to Bösendorfer pianos and performing for heads of state around the world.

Kim Peek

The inspiration behind the movie "Rain Man," Kim Peek was famous for being able to perfectly memorise any book he read. While he did not have the motor skills to button up his own shirt, Peek could perfectly recall the contents of 12,000 books.

Stanley Kubrick

It's been widely speculated that director Stanley Kubrick had Asperger's Syndrome. The director has been described as an "intense, cool, misanthropic cinematic genius who obsesses over every detail." Kubrick's single-minded obsession with filmmaking was so strong that he could only enjoy life when he was standing behind a camera. "I'm happy – at times – making film. I'm certainly unhappy not making films."

Craig Nicholls

Craig Nicholls, frontman of Australian rock band The Vines, was diagnosed with Asperger's Syndrome after being charged with assault for kicking a photographer during a show. When he was let go under the condition that he seek help for his condition, Nicholls shouted out: "I'm free!" When asked if Asperger's was the root of his destructive behaviour, Nicholls told an interviewer: "Yeah, I'd like to say that. That's a good excuse anyway, for acting like a jerk."

Blind Tom Wiggins

Tom Wiggins was a master pianist of the 19th century, who could play anything he heard. Some called him the "human parrot" or the "human phonograph." One of Wiggins' most impressive tricks was playing three songs at once. He could play "Fisher's Hornpipe" with his left hand, "Yankee Doodle" with his right, and sing "Dixie" all at once.

Andy Warhol

Andy Warhol was never diagnosed with autism while he was alive, but autism expert Dr. Judith Gould insists that he "almost certainly had Asperger's syndrome." Warhol's monosyllabic conversational style, meticulously structured routines, and unique creative vision all show strong signs that the legendary artist was on the autism spectrum, Dr. Gould says.

David Byrne

When asked about his condition, Talking Heads frontman David Byrne says that he just sees himself as "different" – not defective. "We all don't have to be the same," Byrne has said. "I used to get annoyed when folks placed value judgements on sociability — implying those who are not gregarious or social are somehow less — it's just different."

Tim Burton

Tim Burton's long-time partner, Helena Bonham-Carter, is convinced that the legendary director has Asperger's. "You start recognizing the signs," she has said. "We were watching a documentary about autism, and he said that was how he felt as a child."

Satoshi Tajiri

The creator of Pokemon, Satoshi Tajiri, has been diagnosed with Asperger's syndrome. His colleagues have described him as "reclusive" and "eccentric" – but his unusual brain is the mastermind behind one of the highest-grossing franchises of all time.

Leslie Lemke

Leslie Lemke struggles with his motor controls so badly that he can't hold onto utensils without dropping them. When he sits down at the piano, though, he can play anything he hears. Lemke's foster parents first realised his talent when they heard him, , sitting down and playing Tchaikovsky's Piano Concerto no. 1 without ever having taken a single piano lesson and after only having heard it once on television.

H.P. Lovecraft

Master of horror, H.P. Lovecraft died before Asperger's syndrome became a recognised diagnosis, but few have been posthumously diagnosed with it as often as he has. Multiple books have been written about Lovecraft's unusual habits. "He certainly displayed all the symptoms," one reads: "A lack of empathy and concern for others, obsessive interests, and a work ethic bordering on the compulsive."

Stephen Wiltshire

Stephen Wiltshire is an artist with the uncanny ability to draw any landscape after only having seen it once.

Dan Harmon

"Rick and Morty" and "Community" creator Dan Harmon has never been formally diagnosed with Asperger's syndrome, but he's convinced that he has it. "I started looking up these symptoms, just to know what they are," he said, "and the more I looked them up, the more familiar they started to seem."

Daniel Tammet

Daniel Tammet made a name for himself when he recited pi from memory to 22,514 digits. His mind, though, is capable of far more incredible things than that. Tammet has the ability to master languages incredibly quickly, once conducting a full interview in Icelandic after only studying the language for a week.

Glenn Gould

Eccentric master pianist Glenn Gould, whose performances were marked by strange habits like rocking and humming while playing the piano, has long been suspected to have had Asperger's syndrome. "Every new hall, every new piano and every new person was extremely stressful to Gould," says Dr. Timothy Maloney, director of the music division of the National Library of Canada. "As he grew older, he needed to be at removed from society. This is an arch example of an Asperger's sufferer."

Jedediah Buxton

Jedediah Buxton couldn't write a word, but he had an incredible ability to do math. In the 18th century, he found work as a human calculator — a man who could sum up any math equation anyone needed, entirely in his head.

Derek Paravicini

Derek Paravicini was born extremely premature at only 25 weeks. He was blind and suffered severe learning disabilities — but he also had absolutely perfect pitch. Paravicini was 9-years-old when he played his first concert with an orchestra. He has played for Princess Diana and been featured on countless shows, usually labeled a "superhuman."

This wide elaboration on famous people living or people who lived with autism spectrum disorder is to give hope to those suffering from the disorder as well as encourage loved ones with the disorder not to lose hope but stay on the right path and follow management procedures. It should equally be kept at the back of the mind that God helps those who make an effort to help themselves. Therefore, diagnosed in any shade of the spectrum gives an even better reason to look up to the Creator and ask Him what he wants of you or how He wants you to impact fellow human beings – just like how the above-mentioned people supposedly did.

Conclusion

This book may not have exploited a centime of the total information about Autism and Asperger's syndrome, but an indispensable framework of knowledge about these disorders has been elaborated here. Parents, guardians and society at large can comfortably acquire knowledge from here and apply it to their daily life to detect and manage children and adults attained with these disorders.

Last words about the book. Research is still going on to shed more light about the disease as well as the non-exhaustive nature of the book on the disease.

Introduction

After writing the book titled *Introduction to Autism and Asperger's syndrome*, there are some questions which we believe straightforward answers can be given. These answers are meant to meet the immediate and superficial needs of those concerned, thus leaving the main book itself a prerequisite to understanding and managing Autism and Asperger's syndrome. This book will, therefore, answer a handful of frequently asked questions as far as these conditions are concerned. The answers provided below will be keys to further research and reading, as they may not be a hundred percent guarantee to meet your quest. The failure to give full reliability is due to the diverse and complex nature of these disease conditions. We equally may not provide the answer in the angle you expect, but we will make sure to simplify it as much as possible for your expectations.

How to get diagnosed

Getting a diagnosis in case of every abnormality and the autism spectrum disorders, in particular, is the ideal decision to make when suspicions of disorder in any form are observed.

1. Talk to someone for advice

If you or your loved one have any signs of autism, the best thing to do is to talk to someone who is quite knowledgeable about it. These people can include:

- A General Practitioner (GP)
- A health visitor (for children under 5)
- Any other health professional, such as another medical practitioner or therapist
- Special educational needs (SENCO) staff at your child's school
- If you are concerned, ask them to refer you for an autism assessment.
- It should be noted that an autism assessment is done by autism specialists. This is the lone recommended way to find out if you or your loved one is autistic or not.
- To make such inquiries, there are things you should and not do.
- What **needs to be done** include:
- Write an elaborate list of the signs of autism you think you or your loved one have and bring it with you.
- Inquire from people who know you or your loved one well (like family, friends or teachers) if they have noticed any possible signs which could be written on the list.
- Come along with didactic material or an easy typing electronic device so you can take notes.
- Do not forget to come along with the loved one concerned or bring along someone who knows enough to be a reliable source of

information. In most cases, this should occur when the second point above has not been validated.

What **should not** be done include:

- Try not to talk too much about other things, as they may be a distraction for a reliable diagnosis – autism and autism-related topics should be the main thing you talk about.

2. Have an autism assessment

An autism assessment is where a team of autism specialists check if you or your loved one is autistic. Like every other assessment team, there are a handful things they are going to do before coming out with a final statement. They include:

- Ask about any problems you or your loved one are having.
- Watch how you or your loved one interact with other people.
- Speak to people who know you or your loved one well, such as family, friends, your general practitioner or your loved one's teachers.

At the end of the assessment, you'll be given a report saying if you or your loved one is autistic.

How can diagnosis help?

Before going in for the diagnosis of autism, you need to know how it could help those concerned. We have established two sets of persons and how diagnosis could help them.

Parents and children

Diagnosis can help to:

- Understand your child's needs and how you can help your child

- Get support for your child at school
- Get support for parents and carers, such as financial benefits
- Understand that your child is not just being "naughty" or "difficult"

Adults

For adults, a diagnosis can help you to:

- Understand why you might find some things harder to do, think or say than other people
- Explain to others why you see and feel the world in a different way
- Get support at college, university or work
- Get some financial benefits

If you find it hard to get diagnosed?

Truth be told; it is not always easy to get an autism assessment. Waiting times can become pretty long. Some reasons behind this delay include the fact the assessment team members are supposed to be available at the same time, so longer waiting times give enough room for programmed availability. At times, the team members want to judge the patient in question to know if the signs and symptoms are clear enough or that the intention is sincere. Nonetheless, if you're finding it hard to get an assessment, you could:

- Ask to speak to someone else, like another general practitioner – this is called getting a second opinion
- Call the National Autistic Society helpline for those in the UK on 0808 800 4104 – they can give you advice about your options, including private assessments
- It may also help to speak to other people who have been in a similar situation

Where do you get support?

Like every other disease, where to get help remains an indispensable question to ask when an autistic patient is involved. Here, we will outline a handful of sources from which help can or must not be sought.

Family and Friends

Family and friends make up the first most popular source of help and advice for Autism and Asperger's syndrome as well as in day to day activities, diseases and abnormalities of every sort.

Telling people close to us about your or your child's autism diagnosis can help them understand what this means. They may, therefore, be able to help in a handful of ways, including:

- Everyday things, so you have more time to focus on yourself or your child and be more productive
- Emotional support plays a key role - as a balanced emotional status ensures better health and better adaptability

National charities

Different countries have different associations or organisations, which take care of people living with inabilities. They possess the adequate infrastructure and knowledge in centres to help guide autistic-related problems as well as a vast majority of others - depending on their scope of operation.

Examples can be:
National Autistic Society in the UK
For parents of autistic children, young autistic people and autistic adults.
Website: www.autism.org.uk
Ambitious about Autism in the UK
For autistic children and young people, their parents and carers.

Website: www.ambitiousaboutautism.org.uk
Autism Awareness Centre in the US;
Website: www.autismawarenesscentre.com

Local support groups

The assessment team that diagnosed you or your child should give you information on local support groups.

You can also search for local groups using:

Social media and forums

There are many people with experience of autism who offer support and share their stories on forums and social media. You do not necessarily have to talk to others in online groups, but it can be pretty helpful to look at what they're saying.

A good place to start is the groups run by autism charities. But bear in mind that health inclined associations do not monitor these sites. Moreover, comments on social media and forums are often based on personal experiences and should not be taken as advice that would fit squarely with you or your child's case. Remember, we also mentioned in the book that there are no all-case-fitting signs or remedies of autism and Asperger's syndrome.

Some groups on social media involve:

Facebook

- National Autistic Society Facebook group
- Ambitious about Autism Facebook group
- Actually Autistic for autistic adults
- Autism Research Trust

Twitter
- <u>National Autistic Society Twitter group</u>
- <u>Ambitious about Autism Twitter group</u>
- <u>Autistica</u>

Forums and communities
- <u>National Autistic Society Community</u>
- <u>Autism Support (HealthUnlocked)</u>

Your school, college or workplace

Your school, college or workplace can be reliable places to acquire information and support as far as autistic cases are concerned.

It is ideal to find out what help is available at the different levels like:

- Nursery or primary school – speak to teachers or special educational needs staff about you or your child's concerns
- College or university – speak to student support services
- Work – speak to your manager and/or human resource personnel

Your local council or local authorities

You can get some support and financial benefits from your local council or local authorities after having expressed your case.

What is available may depend on your situation and specific need.

For children and young people

For people under the age of 25, ask your council about their "local offer."

This is the name for the support they provide for young people with special educational needs, though it may differ from country to country. Therefore, it is a prerequisite that every council has to have a local offer.

You can also get information about the local offer from your local special educational needs advice service.

For adults

If you're an autistic adult or care for an autistic adult, ask your council for a needs assessment or any program set aside by your local authorities for such a purpose.

This is an assessment to find out:

- What problems you're having on a day to day life
- What support or financial benefits you might be able to get

For parents and carers

If you look after someone who's autistic, ask your council for a carer's assessment or any program meant for the same purpose.

This is an assessment to find out what support or financial benefits you might be able to get to help you care for an autistic person.

General practitioners (GPs) and autism assessment teams

If you think you or your child needs help from a health professional, speak to a GP or the assessment team that diagnosed you or the child.

They may be able to refer you to a specialist who can help, such as:

- An occupational therapist
- A mental health specialist
- A speech and language therapist

What are the signs of autism in adults?

Main signs of autism

Common signs of autism in adults include:

- Finding it hard to understand what others are thinking or feeling
- Getting very anxious about social situations
- Finding it hard to make friends or preferring to be on your own
- Seeming blunt, rude or not interested in others without meaning to
- Finding it difficult to say how you feel
- Taking things very literally – for example, you may not understand jokes or phrases like "It is raining cats and dogs"
- Having the same routine every day and getting very anxious or even angry if it changes

Other signs of autism

You may also have other signs, including:

- Not understanding social "rules," such as not talking over people or not sitting when a pregnant woman stands
- Avoiding eye contact
- Getting too close to other people, or getting very upset if someone touches or gets too close to you
- Noticing small details, patterns, smells or sounds that others do not
- Having a very keen interest in certain subjects or activities
- Liking to plan things carefully before executing them

How is Autism in women compared to men?

As stated in the book, *Introduction to Autism and Asperger's syndrome,* Autism can sometimes be different in women and men. For example, autistic women may be quieter, may hide their feelings and may appear to cope better with social situations. This means it can be harder to tell you're autistic if you're a woman.

For women, it is advisable to tell a GP if you think you may be autistic.

If you already see a health professional, such as another doctor or therapist, you could speak to them instead. It is always important to note that getting diagnosed can help you get any extra support you might need.

Based on the statistics from *Introduction to Autism and Asperger's syndrome*, the average onset age is about 7 years old. Boys are more likely to be diagnosed with autism than girls.

What is the difference between Autism Spectrum Disorder and ADHD?

Behaviours associated with autism spectrum disorder can look a lot like attention deficit hyperactivity disorder (ADHD). Here's an overview of signs and symptoms, plus common reasons why parents miss ASD. Some parents wonder whether their child with ADHD may have some form of autism.

To be more elaborate on these differences, we run through the signs of autism spectrum disorder. They include:

- Learning disability
- Attention deficit hyperactivity disorder (ADHD) Tourette's syndrome or other tic disorders
- Epilepsy
- Dyspraxia
- Obsessive compulsive disorder (OCD) generalised anxiety disorder
- Depression

From the signs above, we see that though ADHD is a disorder on its own, it is subordinated to ASD.

Similar to ASD, attention deficit hyperactivity disorder affects children and teens and can continue into adulthood. ADHD is the most commonly diagnosed mental disorder of children. Children with ADHD may be hyperactive and unable to control their impulses or have trouble paying attention.

The signs include:

- Being unable to sit still, especially in calm or quiet surroundings
- Constantly fidgeting
- Being unable to concentrate on tasks
- Excessive physical movement
- Excessive talking
- Being unable to wait their turn
- Acting without thinking
- Interrupting conversations

Conclusively, Autism spectrum disorder and ADHD are related in several ways. ADHD is not on the autism spectrum, but it have some of the same symptoms. ... The fourth edition of the Diagnostic and Statistical Manual of Mental Disorders (DSM-IV) stated that a person couldn't have autism and ADHD because the latter is a sign of Autism.

Can a child with autism have ADHD?

As mentioned earlier, there may be a reason why ADHD and ASD symptoms can be difficult to distinguish. Both can occur at the same time. A doctor may decide only one of the disorders is responsible for your child's symptoms. Not every child can be clearly diagnosed.

What is the difference between autism and Asperger's syndrome?

After a keen reading of my book Introduction *to Autism and Asperger's Syndrome*, the diagnosis of an autism spectrum disorder is important because it explains and shades understanding both on similarities and differences between disorders on the spectrum. Asperger's Syndrome and high functioning autism (HFA) are often referred to as the same diagnosis.

What are the different types of autism?

There are three types of autism spectrum disorders classified from the most severe to the less severe cases.

Autistic Disorder

This is sometimes called "classic" autism. It is what most people think of when they hear the word "autism." People with autistic disorder usually have significant language delays, social and communication challenges, and unusual behaviours and interests. Many people with autistic disorder also have intellectual disability.

Asperger's Syndrome

People with Asperger's syndrome usually possess milder symptoms of autistic disorder. They might have social challenges and unusual behaviours and interests. However, they typically do not have problems with language or intellectual disability.

Pervasive Developmental Disorder – Not Otherwise Specified

This is sometimes called "atypical autism," or PDD-NOS. Here, we have people who meet some of the criteria for autistic disorder or Asperger's syndrome, but not all may be diagnosed with atypical autism. These people usually have fewer and milder symptoms than those with autistic disorder. The symptoms might cause only social and communication challenges.

What does it mean to have a child on the spectrum?

"On the spectrum" usually refers to the specific set of behavioural and developmental problems as well as the challenges associated with autism spectrum disorder. A diagnosis of ASD means that your child's communication, social, and play skills are affected somehow. To add to the confusion, experts use different names to describe ASD.

What is the definition of ADD and ADHD?

The medical ***Definition of ADD*** (***attention deficit disorder***): ***ADHD*** is a common condition that affects ***children*** and adolescents, while ***ADD*** is more common in adults.

What are ADHD symptoms in children?

According to NHS, the symptoms of ADHD in children and teenagers are well defined and usually noticeable before the age of 6. They occur in more than one situation, such as at home and school.

Inattentiveness

The main signs of inattentiveness are:

- Having a short attention span and being easily distracted
- Making careless mistakes – for example, in schoolwork
- Appearing forgetful or losing things
- Being unable to stick to tasks that are tedious or time-consuming
- Appearing to be unable to listen to or carry out instructions
- Constantly changing activity or task
- Difficulty organising tasks

Hyperactivity and impulsiveness

The main signs of hyperactivity and impulsiveness are:

- Being unable to sit still, especially in calm or quiet surroundings
- Constantly fidgeting
- Unable to concentrate on tasks
- Excessive physical movement
- Excessive talking
- Unable to wait their turn
- Acting without thinking
- Interrupting conversations
- Little or no sense of danger

These symptoms can cause significant problems in a child's life, such as underachievement at school, poor social interaction with other children and adults, and problems with discipline.

Is Asperger's ADD?

Asperger's syndrome and ADD are two conditions that both involve brain development. They tend to develop early in life and may cause some similar behavioural traits. The medical community, as of 2013, no longer diagnose Asperger's syndrome as a separate condition.

Which other conditions affect autistic people?

Attention deficit hyperactivity disorder (ADHD)

The symptoms of ADHD include:

- Finding it hard to concentrate and getting distracted easily
- Acting without thinking
- Finding it hard to sit still

People with ADHD may need extra support at school or work. Sometimes, they need to take medicine.

Dyslexia and dyspraxia

Some autistic people have:

- Problems with reading, writing and spelling (dyslexia)

- Clumsy movements and problems with organisation and following instructions (dyspraxia)

Extra support at school can often help.

Problems sleeping (insomnia)

The symptoms of insomnia include:

- Finding it hard to go to sleep
- Waking up several times during the night
- Waking up early and not being able to go back to sleep

Changing your bedtime routine can often help.

Find out more about sleep problems from the National Autistic Society.

Mental health problems

Many autistic people have problems like:

- Feeling very worried a lot of the time (anxiety)
- Feeling unhappy, irritable or hopeless (depression)
- Feeling a need to keep doing certain actions (obsessive compulsive disorder, or OCD)

These conditions can often be treated with talking therapies or medicines.

Learning disabilities

A person with a learning disability may find it hard to:

- Understand new or complicated information
- Learn new skills
- Look after themselves

People with a learning disability often need help with daily life.

Epilepsy

Symptoms of epilepsy include:

- Shaking and collapsing (called a "fit" or seizure)
- Staring blankly into space
- Strange smells or tastes
- Tingling in your arms or legs

Epilepsy can often be treated with medicine.

Problems with joints and other parts of the body

Some autistic people may have:

- Flexible or painful joints
- Skin that stretches or bruises easily
- Diarrhoea or constipation that does not go away

These can be caused by conditions like joint hypermobility syndrome or Ehlers-Danlos syndromes.

You may need support from a range of health professionals, including a physiotherapist.

What should the newly diagnosed do?

Give yourself time

People react to a diagnosis of autism in different ways.

For some, it's a relief to find out why they or their child think, feel and act the way they do. For others, it can be a shock.

Try to give yourself time to come to terms with the diagnosis.

Remember:

- Help and support is available
- Even if things are hard now, they can get better
- You or your child are still the same person as before
- Autism is not an illness or disease with treatments or a "cure"
- Autistic people have things they're good at as well as things they need help with

Can a person with Asperger's or Autism feel love?

Despite the problems in relationship skills experienced by many **people with Asperger's** syndrome, some adults **can** progress along the relationship continuum and experience romantic and subsequently intimate personal relationships, even becoming a lifelong partner.

What causes Asperger syndrome?

Genetics. Several different genes appear to be involved in **autism** spectrum disorder. For some children, **autism** spectrum disorder can be associated with a genetic disorder, such as Rett syndrome or fragile X syndrome. For other children, genetic changes (mutations) may increase the risk of **autism** spectrum disorder.

What is the life expectancy of someone with Asperger's?

One study published in the American Journal of Public Health in April 2017 finds the **life expectancy** in the United States of those with ASD to be 36 years old compared to 72 years old for the general population. They note that those with ASD are 40 times more likely to die from various injuries.

Do Asperger's get angry?

In addition to difficulties with understanding emotions, individuals with ASDs may **become angry** quickly and may **have** difficulty calming themselves effectively. They often need to be taught skills to cope with an increase in irritability once they **have** been able to identify these emotions.

How do you talk to someone with Asperger's?

Think positive, don't take immediate offence at misaligned words, body language or tone of voice. Check and ask what the other **person** means in order to maintain clear communication. Don't think the worst, don't mistake frustration or anxiety in others for them being angry with you.

What happens if Asperger's goes untreated?

Some of the effects of unaddressed or **untreated Asperger's** syndrome may include social isolation, difficulty making and keeping friends and challenges in finding and maintaining steady employment.

Can you outgrow Asperger's?

Research in the past several years has shown that children **can outgrow** a diagnosis of autism spectrum disorder (ASD), once considered a lifelong condition. In a new study, researchers have found that the vast majority of such children still have difficulties that require therapeutic and educational support.

Can someone have mild Asperger's?

People with the disorder are said to fall somewhere along the "autism spectrum." Some are severely disabled, but others may only exhibit mild symptoms. IQ levels can also vary significantly. Those with normal and above-average intelligence are said to have high-functioning autism.

Is Asperger's considered a disability?

A child with an **Asperger's** diagnosis and impaired social, personal, or cognitive functioning may qualify for **disability** benefits.

Do Asperger's have empathy?

Do people with **Asperger's have empathy**? Contrary to popular belief, people with **Asperger's do have empathy**. They care about how others are thinking and feeling, but they often **have** difficulty putting themselves in other people's shoes. This is a skill that can be learned over time.

Do Asperger's feel lonely?

Some children with **Asperger** syndrome find mainstream education difficult. Some find that bullying is an issue, that they **feel lonely** or are unable to keep up with their peers.

What is the best medication for Asperger's?

There is no one treatment for autism, and autism does not mean anything is wrong with you that needs to be cured. Treatment generally focuses on managing **autism symptoms** — for instance, learning how to better communicate and reducing any repetitive behaviours that interfere with your life. Treatment options can include therapies and medications.

Therapies

Behaviour therapies address the social and behavioural issues that can cause distress for people with autism and interfere with their relationships. Family therapy can help family members learn the best way to interact with family members who have autism.

Speech or language therapy may be beneficial to help with issues like monotone speech. It may also help with understanding figures of speech and implied meaning. Occupational therapy can help with sensory integration, and physical therapy may be helpful with balance and coordination issues.

Medications

There is no medication that can treat the core characteristics of autism, but there are medications that can help with some symptoms. Certain medications can be prescribed for the **hyperactivity** that some autistic people experience, for example. **Antidepressants** may help with **anxiety**. It's important to keep all doctors involved up to date on all medications since some can interact and cause adverse effects.

Special diets

Maintaining a healthy **diet** is important for people with autism. Children with autism have been shown to have thinner bones than children without autism. While some people promote **gluten**-free or casein-free diets to treat autism, there is no evidence that these approaches work. In addition, these diets may limit bone-building foods, causing harm.

Possible complications and side effects

The medications used to treat some **symptoms of autism** can have adverse effects. Discuss any new medications with your doctor, and let a medical professional know if you've been feeling worse since starting a new medication.

Antidepressant side effects can include:

- **Insomnia**
- **Indigestion**
- **Sexual dysfunction**
- **Headaches**

Additionally, antidepressants in children can trigger feelings of hostility, **anxiety**, and **impulsivity**, along with **suicidal thoughts**.

Stimulants are often used to treat hyperactivity and inability to focus in people with autism. Stimulant side effects can include:

- **Anxiety**
- **Sleep problems**
- **Loss of appetite**
- **Weight loss**
- **Agitation**

How does an Asperger's mind work?

The information below is a direct extract from the NCBI website. It has a conversational approach to this question and gives a clear insight as well.

ABSTRACT

"My mind is similar to an Internet search engine that searches for photographs. I use language to narrate the photo-realistic pictures that pop up in my imagination. When I design equipment for the cattle industry, I can test run it in my imagination similar to a virtual reality computer program. All my thinking is associative and not linear. To form concepts, I sort pictures into categories similar to computer files. To form the concept of orange, I see many different orange objects, such as oranges, pumpkins, orange juice and marmalade. I have observed that there are three different specialised autistic/Asperger cognitive types. They are: (i) visual thinkers such as I who are often poor at algebra, (ii) pattern thinkers, such as Daniel Tammet, who excel in math and music but may have problems with reading or writing composition, and (iii) verbal specialists who are good at talking and writing but lack visual skills.

Keywords: *visual thinking, imagination, autobiography, photo-realistic memory*

1. INTRODUCTION

My mind works similar to an Internet search engine, set to locate photos. All my thoughts are in photo-realistic pictures, which flash up on the 'computer monitor' in my imagination. Words just narrate the picture. When I design livestock facilities, I can test run the equipment in my imagination similar to a virtual reality computer program. I did not know that this was a special skill until I started interviewing other people about how they think. I was surprised to discover that the other non-autistic equipment designers could not do full motion test runs of equipment in their minds.

My mind is associative and does not think in a linear manner. If you say the word 'butterfly,' the first picture I see is butterflies in my childhood backyard. The next image is metal decorative butterflies that people decorate the outside of their houses with, and the third image is some butterflies I painted on a piece of plywood when I was in graduate school. Then my mind gets off the subject and I see a butterfly cut of chicken that was served at a fancy restaurant approximately three days ago. The memories that come up first tend to be either early childhood or something that happened within the last week. A teacher working with a child with autism may not understand the connection when the child suddenly switches from talking about butterflies to talking about chicken. If the teacher thinks about it visually, a butterfly cut of chicken looks like a butterfly.

2. PUTTING LITTLE PIECES TOGETHER

When I design equipment, I take bits and pieces of other equipment I have seen in the past and combine them to create a new system. All my thinking is bottom-up instead of top-down. I find lots of little details and put them together to form concepts and theories.

During the last 5 years, I successfully used this method to fix some of my health problems. Most people have to have a theory first, and then they try to make the data conform to it. My mind works the opposite way. I put lots of little pieces of data together to form a new theory. I read lots of journal papers, and I take little pieces of information and put them together as if completing a jigsaw puzzle. Imagine if you had a thousand-piece jigsaw puzzle in a paper bag, and you had no idea what the picture on the box is? When you start to put the puzzle together, you will be able to see what the picture is when it is approximately one-third or one-quarter of the way completed. When I solve the problem, it is not top-down and theory driven. Instead, I look at how all the little pieces fit together to form a bigger picture.

When I was in college, I called this finding the basic principle. On everything in life, I was overwhelmed with a mass of details, and I realised that I had to group them together and try to figure out unifying principles for masses of data.

3. FINDING A UNIFYING PRINCIPLE IN SCIENTIFIC LITERATURE

I have recently started to lose my hearing. The ear specialist said that there was nothing I could do. I did not accept this; so I spent two weeks at the computer reading journal papers on sudden sensorial hearing loss, Meniere's disease and other disorders. I had to read hundreds of abstracts and journal papers just to get the background information so that I could find the answer that would save my hearing. I was looking for a unifying principle that would explain all the research results. One study reported that steroids, such as Prednisone, could save my hearing, and another study reported that steroids do not work. How did I sort the data out? The first clue was that many studies were published in arthritis journals instead of ear and nose journals. The reason for this is that arthritis doctors really understand autoimmune disorders where the immune system attacks a person's body. In my mind, I pictured wrecked, deformed arthritic joints. For a treatment to be successful, the drug has to be given before the immune system has destroyed the joints. I then had a flash of visual thinking insight. I imagined that the immune system attacking my inner ear was such as a house on fire. This is what I call a visual symbol picture. If the fire is put out when it is confined to a waste basket, the house can be saved. If the whole house starts burning, it will be destroyed. The explanation for all the conflicting studies in the medical journals was really simple. Steroid drugs, such as Prednisone, put out the fire of autoimmune inflammation, but they do not repair the damage. Treatment has to be started before the ear is wrecked. The explanation for all the conflicting scientific studies was a simple basic principle. I had to get a prescription for Prednisone before the autoimmune inflammation destroyed my inner ear. I looked up a second ear specialist in the phone book, and he immediately gave me the prescription that saved my hearing.

4. FILLING UP THE INTERNET IN MY MIND

The method of bottom-up thinking really works well for me in problem-solving where a basic principle has to be determined from masses of conflicting data. One disadvantage of my kind of thinking is that huge amounts of data are required to find the answers. Since my mind works similar to an Internet search engine, my ability to solve problems got better and better as I had more and more experiences and read more and more books and journal papers. This provided lots of images in my memory for the search engine in my mind to search. Many people have told me that my talks have improved between the ages of 40 and 60. My ability to think in a less rigid way keeps getting better as I fill up the Internet in my mind with more and more information. I greatly improved socially in my 40s and 50s compared with my 20s. This was due to having more experiences in my memory that provided guidance on how to behave.

5. DOOR SYMBOLS

When I was in high school at age 16, many teachers did not understand why I kept talking about going through little doors and thinking in visual symbols. Since my mind stores information as photo-realistic pictures, I do not have true abstract thinking. To visualise the concept of my future after high school, I had to use door symbols. In fact, the first door symbols were real doors I could practise walking through. Today, I no longer think in door symbols because I have a huge database in the Internet inside my head. Instead of visualizing doors, I visualise either real past experiences or events I have read about.

6. CATEGORIES ARE THE BEGINNING OF CONCEPT FORMATION

To form a concept from the many specific photo-realistic pictures I have stored in my memory, I sort them into categories. Categorization of my specific visual memories was the beginning of concept formation (Grandin 2000, 2002). When I was a child, I categorised dogs from cats by sorting the animals by sise. All the dogs in our neighbourhood were large until our neighbours got a Dachshund. I remember looking at the small dog and trying to figure out why she was not a cat. I had to find a visual feature that she shared with big dogs. I had to create a new category in my mind to differentiate. All dogs, no matter how big or small, have the same nose shape. My concept is sensory based, not word based. Other ways of sensory-based categorization would be sound (barking or meowing) or smell.

Researchers have found that people with autism often have difficulty in forming new categories (Minshew et al., 2002). When I was a child, we played lots of games, such as Twenty Questions, that forced me to get good at thinking in categories. Category formation is a fundamental property of the nervous system. Brains are wired to put visual information into categories (Freedman et al., 2001). The hippocampus also has the ability to determine whether or not similar photos of objects are the same or different (Bakker et al., 2008). Observations of stroke patients have shown that brain damage can cause them to lose their ability to categorise objects such as tools, but they can still categorise vegetables and animals (e.g. Mummery et al., 1998).

In my case even abstract questions are answered by putting photo-realistic pictures into categories. One time, I was asked 'Is capitalism a good system?' To answer this question, I put pictures from countries that had different types of governmental systems into the following categories: (i) capitalistic, (ii) capitalistic/socialistic, (iii) socialistic, (iv) benevolent dictatorship, (v) brutal dictatorship, and (vi) war and chaos. These pictures were taken from my memory and they are from experiences travelling or the news media. My answer was that I absolutely do not want to live in a brutal dictatorship, or war and chaos. Pictures helped me make a choice because in the last two choices, I see news photos and TV images of killing and destruction.

My ability to provide a well thought-out answer has greatly improved with age because I have travelled more and have more pictures from actual experiences and from reading. They can be sorted into the different categories. When I read, I convert text to images as if watching a movie. The images are then stored in my memory. In college, I photocopied images of my class notes into my brain. When I was a teenager, answering the question about capitalism in an intelligent manner would have been impossible. I simply did not have enough experiences or enough information in my memory to answer it.

7. HOW I DEVELOPED FASTER CATEGORY THINKING

In college, the process of sorting out the basic principles from masses of data was much slower and laborious compared with my abilities today at 60. I figured out my ear problem in two weeks. When I was in my 20s, it took me 10 times longer to develop a theory from 100 journal papers.

As an undergraduate, I did an Honour's thesis on the subject of sensory interaction. Here the question was how a stimulus to one sense, such as hearing, affects the sensitivity of other senses. I had over 100 journal papers and I numbered each paper. On small pieces of paper, I typed the major findings of each study. I then pinned hundreds of little slips of paper on a bulletin board. I called it my logic board. Since my thinking is totally non-sequential, I had to develop a way so I could see a display of all the information at the same time on the bulletin board. To discover the categories and concepts, I started pinning the slips of paper into different categories. It was very time-consuming. As I gained more experience with sifting through scientific research, I no longer needed the bulletin board. I became better and better at finding unexpected clues, such as many deafness treatment papers being in arthritis journals. From my previous scientific knowledge, I made the association of rheumatoid arthritis to autoimmune, and therefore saw that ear damage would work the same way as joint damage.

When I was young, my thinking process was extremely slow because I was less skilled at finding the basic principle from the masses of data. But skills in people on the autism spectrum still develop when they are adults. The more research I did analysing the results of scientific studies, the better I got at it. I always read the methods section of a paper carefully so I can visualise how the experiment was done. Differences in methods often explain conflicting results of scientific studies.

8. DIFFERENT WAYS OF THINKING

For many years, I thought everybody else thought in pictures the same way as I do. When I wrote Thinking in Pictures, I started interviewing people about how they think. I was shocked to learn that most people processed information differently to how I did. Most people are able to visualise their own car or visualise walking through their own house. They can do it because they are very familiar with it. I discovered the differences in thinking when I asked other people about objects they were less familiar with. I asked them about an object that everybody sees really often, but it was not visible when I asked the question. I always ask the question in the exact way, so I do not bias the answer. 'Access your memory of church steeples. How do they come into your mind?' I was shocked to discover that many people saw a vague generalised steeple, and sometimes it was a stick figure. They saw a generalised steeple where I saw only a whole lot of photo-realistic pictures of specific ones that I could identify. Research by Nancy Minshew and her colleagues has shown that in people with autism, word-based tasks are processed in the visual parts of the brain. Functional magnetic resonance imaging scanning indicated that sentences with both high and low visual imageries were processed in the visual parts of the brain in the autistic subjects and that low visual imagery sentences were processed in the language parts of the brain in normal subjects (Kana et al., 2006). The sentences with high visual imagery were about animals and plants. One of the low visual imagery sentences was about arithmetic. When I did the experiment, I instantly saw my third-grade teacher writing on the blackboard and explaining borrowing in subtraction.

9. AUTISTIC THINKING IS SPECIALISED

When I wrote Thinking in Pictures (Grandin 1995) I thought everybody on the autism/Asperger spectrum was a visual thinker. People with autism and Asperger's are specialist thinkers. They are good at one thing and bad at other things. From both books and interviews, I have concluded that there are three principal types of specialist thinking.

10. DIFFERENT KINDS OF BRAINS

Recent research on the white matter in the brain may provide an explanation for the uneven profile of abilities that is found in many individuals with autism. There are defects in the white matter interconnections between different localised brain regions. Courchesne et al. (2004) called these connections the 'computer cables' that wire different parts of the brain together. The frontal cortex gets less connections than other parts of the brain, but some local areas in the brain may get extra connections (Minshew & Williams, 2007). Casanova and colleagues (2006, 2007; Casanova & Trippe, 2009) found that the brain of both famous neuroscientists and people on the autism spectrum have more circuits (mini-columns) per square centimetre of brain. They suggest that this may explain savant-like skills. The disadvantage of this type of brain construction is that these small circuits have fewer long-distance connections between distant brain regions that facilitate complex social behaviours. There is a wide range of brains that should be considered part of normal variation. A brain can be built with larger fast circuits that facilitate social communication or smaller, slower circuits that improve cognition in a specialised area.

In any information processing system, there are always trade-offs. Brains with high-speed connections to many distant areas will be fast, and details will be missed. Research shows that normal brains fail to process details that the autistic person perceives (see Happé & Frith, 2009; Happé & Vital, 2009). My model for visualizing the different types of brains is a large corporate office building. The president (frontal cortex) is located at the top, and he has telephone and computer connections (white matter) to offices throughout the building. I hypothesise that in a highly social brain, the frontal cortex has high-speed connections that go mainly to the department heads in the building. The network is fast, and details are omitted. In the autistic/Asperger brain, the frontal cortex is poorly connected, but the visual and auditory parts of the brain (technical nerd departments) have lots of extra local connections providing better processing of detailed information.

11. AUTISTIC INTELLIGENCE

Michelle Dawson, a woman with autism, has teamed up with Laurent Mottron, a researcher in Canada, to show that autistic intelligence goes beyond just rote memorization. Instead of using just the Wechsler IQ tests, they tested both normal and autistic children with Raven's Progressive Matrices (Dawson et al., 2007). In this test, the person is shown complicated patterns, and he/she has to choose the pattern that will complete a series of patterns. Dawson and colleagues found that the IQ scores for the autistic children were 30–70 percentile points higher on the Raven's compared with the Wechsler Intelligence Scale for Children (WISC), while normal children have similar IQ scores when given the Raven's and the WISC. Scheuffgen et al. (2000) found that children with autism can show fast information processing despite poor measured IQ. These results show that autistic intelligence is truly different.

In 2006, Nancy Minshew and her colleagues performed a method called diffusion tensor imaging on me. They found a huge white fibre tract that runs from deep in my visual cortex up to my frontal cortex. It is located in the brain slice made at the level of my eyes. It is almost twice as large as my sex- and age-matched controls. I used to joke about having a big high-speed Internet line deep in my visual cortex. It turned out that I really do have one. This may explain my ability to read massive amounts of detailed literature and sort out the details. In my case, abstract thought based on language has been replaced with high-speed handling of hundreds of 'graphics' files. Studies of patients with frontotemporal dementia show that language-based thinking can cover up detailed visual thinking and music. As the disease destroys the frontal lobe and the language parts of the brain, art and music talent can emerge in people who had no previous interest in art or music (Miller et al., 1998, 2000; see also Snyder, 2009).

12. HARNESSING AUTISTIC CREATIVITY AND ASPERGER'S SYNDROME

I am concerned that people with mild Asperger's syndrome may be held back by the diagnosis because people may perceive them as not capable. Simon Baron-Cohen asks 'is Asperger's syndrome a disability?' (Baron-Cohen 2000; see also Baron-Cohen et al., 2009). Many famous musicians, scientists, artists and politicians would probably be diagnosed with Asperger's syndrome if they were children today (Ledgin, 2002; Fitzgerald & O'Brien, 2007). What would happen to them in today's system? In the USA, the lucky ones get apprenticed into the Silicon Valley technical world by their parents. Many parents in technical fields teach their children their jobs at a young age. The unlucky ones do not have somebody to help them develop their skills. In countries, such as China or India, a person with mild Asperger's syndrome would go to engineering or computer science school. I have discussed this with parents from India or East Asia, and they stress working with the child from a young age in career-relevant skills. We need to be working to develop the unique abilities of these individuals. I am worried about them getting 'stuck in a rut,' and their creative skills will not be used."

What jobs are good for someone with Asperger's?

This extract from Temple Grandin, Ph.D. Assistant Professor Colorado State University Fort Collins, CO 80523, USA (November, 1999) sheds more light on this question.

"Jobs need to be chosen that make use of the strengths of people with autism or Asperger's syndrome. Both high and low functioning people have very poor short-term working memory, but they often have a better long-term memory than most normal people. I have great difficulty with tasks that put high demands on short-term working memory. I cannot handle multiple tasks at the same time. Table 1 is a list of BAD jobs that I would have great difficulty doing. Table 2 is a list of easy jobs for a visual thinker like me. I have difficulty doing abstract math, such as algebra, and most of the jobs on Table 2 do not require complex math. Many of the visual thinking jobs would also be good for people with dyslexia.

The visual thinking jobs on Table 2 put very little demand on fast processing of information in short-term working memory. They would fully utilise my visual thinking and large long-term memory. Table 3 is a list of jobs that non-visual thinkers who are good with numbers, facts and music could do easily. They also put low demands on short-term working *memory and utilise an excellent long-term memory. Table 4 shows jobs that lower functioning people with autism could do well. For all types of autism and Asperger's syndrome, demands on short-term working memory must be kept low. If I were a computer, I would have a huge hard drive that could hold 10 times as much information as an ordinary computer but my processor chip would be small. To use 1999 computer terminology, I have a 1000 gigabyte hard drive and a little 286 processor. Normal people may have only 10 gigabytes of disc space on their hard drive and a Pentium for a processor. I cannot do two or three things at once.*

Some job tips for people with autism or Asperger's syndrome:

- Jobs should have a well-defined goal or endpoint.
- Sell your work, not your personality. Make a portfolio of your work.
- The boss must recognise your social limitations.

It is important that high functioning autistics and Asperger's syndrome people pick a college major in an area where they can get jobs. Computer science is a good choice because it is very likely that many of the best programmers have either Asperger's syndrome or some of its traits. Other good majors are: accounting, engineering, library science, and art with an emphasis on commercial art and drafting. Majors in history, political science, business, English or pure math should be avoided. However, one could major in library science with a minor in history, but the library science degree makes it easier to get a good job.

Some individuals while they are still in high school should be encouraged to take courses at a local college in drafting, computer programming or commercial art. This will help keep them motivated and serve as a refuge from teasing. Families with low income may be wondering how they can afford computers for their child to learn programming or computer aided drafting. Used computers can often be obtained for free or at a very low cost when a business or an engineering company upgrades their equipment. Many people do not realise that there are many usable older computers sitting in storerooms at schools, banks, factories and other businesses. It will not be the latest new thing, but it is more than adequate for a student to learn on.

In conclusion: a person with Asperger's syndrome or autism has to compensate for poor social skills by making themselves so good in a specialised field that people will be willing to "buy" their skill, even though their social skills are poor. This is why making a portfolio of your work is so important. You need to learn a few social survival skills, but you will make friends at work by sharing your shared interest with the other people who work in your specialty. My social life is almost all work-related. I am friends with people I do interesting work with.

Table 1

Bad Jobs for People with High Functioning Autism or Asperger's Syndrome: Jobs that require high demands on short-term working memory

- *Cashier -- making change quickly puts too much demand on short-term working memory*
- *Short order cook -- Have to keep track of many orders and cook many different things at the same time*
- *Waitress -- Especially difficult if you have to keep track of many different tables*
- *Casino dealer -- Too many things to keep track of*
- *Taxi dispatcher -- Too many things to keep track of*
- *Taking oral dictation -- Difficult due to auditory processing problems*
- *Airline ticket agent -- Deal with angry people when flights are cancelled*
- *Future market trader -- Totally impossible*
- *Air traffic controller -- Information overload and stress*
- *Receptionist and telephone operator -- Would have problems when the switchboard got busy*

Table 2

<u>Good Jobs for Visual Thinkers</u>

- *Computer programming -- Wide-open field with many jobs available, especially in industrial automation, software design, business computers, communications and network systems*

- *Drafting -- Engineering drawings and computer aided drafting. This job can offer many opportunities. Drafting is an excellent portal of entry for many interesting technical jobs. I know people who started out at a company doing drafting and then moved into designing and laying out entire factories. To become really skilled at drafting, one needs to learn how to draw by hand first. I have observed that most of the people who draw beautiful drawings on a computer learned to draw by hand first. People who never learn to draw by hand first tend to leave important details out of their drawings.*

- *Commercial art -- Advertising and magazine layout can be done as freelance work*

- *Photography -- Still and video, TV cameraman can be done as freelance work*

- *Equipment designing -- Many industries, often a person starts as a draftsman and then moves into designing factory equipment*

- *Animal trainer or veterinary technician -- Dog obedience trainer, behaviour problem consultant*

- *Automobile mechanic -- Can visualise how the entire car works*

- *Computer-troubleshooter and repair -- Can visualise problems in computers and networks*

- *Small appliance and lawnmower repair -- Can make a nice local business*

- *Handcrafts of many different types, such as wood carving, jewelry making, ceramics, etc.*

- *Laboratory technician -- Who modifies and builds specialised lab equipment*

- *Web page design -- Find a good niche market can be done as freelance work*

- *Building trades -- Carpenter or welder. These jobs make good use of visual skills but some people will not be able to do them well due to motor and coordination problems.*

- *Video game designer -- Stay out of this field. Jobs are scarce, and the field is overcrowded. There are many more jobs in industrial, communications business and software design computer programming. Another bad thing about this job is exposure to violent images.*

- *Computer animation -- Visual thinkers would be very good at this field, but there is more competition in this field than in business or industrial computer programming. Businesses are recruiting immigrants from overseas because there is a shortage of good programmers in business and industrial fields.*

- *Building maintenance -- Fixes broken pipes, windows and other things in an apartment complex, hotel or office building*

- *Factory maintenance -- Repairs and fixes factory equipment*

Table 3

Good Jobs for Non-Visual Thinkers: Those who are good at math, music or facts

- *Accounting -- Get very good in a specialised field, such as income taxes*
- *Library science -- reference librarian. Help people find information in the library or on the Internet.*
- *Computer programming -- Less visual types can be done as freelance work*
- *Engineering -- Electrical, electronic and chemical engineering*
- *Journalist -- Very accurate facts, can be done as freelance*

- *Copy editor -- Corrects manuscripts. Many people freelance for larger publishers*
- *Taxi driver -- Knows where every street is*
- *Inventory control -- Keeps track of merchandise stocked in a store*
- *Tuning pianos and other musical instruments, can be done as freelance work*
- *Laboratory technician -- Running laboratory equipment*
- *Bank Teller -- Very accurate money counting, much less demand on short-term working memory than a busy cashier who mostly makes change quickly*
- *Clerk and filing jobs -- knows where every file is*
- *Telemarketing -- Get to repeat the same thing over and over, selling on the telephone. Noisy environment may be a problem. Telephone sales avoids many social problems.*
- *Statistician -- Work in many different fields, such as research, census bureau, industrial quality control, U.S. Dept. of Agriculture, etc.*
- *Physicist or mathematician -- There are very few jobs in these fields. Only the very brilliant can get and keep jobs. Jobs are much more plentiful in computer programming and accounting.*

Table 4

Jobs for Nonverbal People with Autism or People with Poor Verbal Skills

- *Reshelving library books -- Can memorise the entire numbering system and shelf locations*

- *Factory assembly work -- Especially if the environment is quiet*

- *Copy shop -- Running photocopies. Printing jobs should be lined up by somebody else*

- *Janitor jobs -- Cleaning floors, toilets, windows and offices*

- *Restocking shelves -- In many types of stores*

- *Recycling plant -- Sorting jobs*

- *Warehouse -- Loading trucks, stacking boxes*

- *Lawn and garden work -- Mowing lawns and landscaping work*

- *Data entry -- If the person has fine motor problems, this would be a bad job*

- *Fast food restaurant -- Cleaning and cooking jobs with little demand on short-term memory*

- *Plant care -- Water plants in a large office building*

Does Asperger's get worse with age?

Goldsmiths, University of London researchers, working with adults recently diagnosed with autism spectrum disorder, have found high rates of depression, low employment, and an apparent worsening of some ASD traits as people age.

Is it hard to date someone with Asperger's?

Dating isn't easy, and it's even less so when you've got Asperger's, an autism spectrum disorder that can make it hard to read social cues.

How do you calm down someone with Asperger's?

Make space - try to create a quiet, safe space as best you can. Ask people to move along and not stare, turn off loud music and turn **down** bright lights – whatever you can think of to reduce the information overload, try it.

How do you help someone with Asperger's?

Social skills training can **help someone with Asperger's** understand social and conversation cues and **help** them to interact with others more effectively. Physical or occupational therap can **help** to improve motor skills in **people with Asperger's** who have problems with coordination.

Do I have autism or am I just socially awkward?

Autism spectrum disorder is primarily characterised by impaired **social** interaction and limited **social**-emotional reciprocity. This impairment goes well beyond poor **social** skills and being **socially awkward**. Children **with autism** spectrum disorder tend to **have** a disconnection in their response to others.

Can you drive a car if you have Asperger's?

One symptom of **Asperger** Syndrome (ASD) **is** an inflexible adherence to rules and order. On the **one** hand, this **could** make a driver **with Asperger** Syndrome (ASD) quite safe -- **they** won't exceed the speed limit or run a red light. However, consider **your** teen's ability to understand some nuance.

What is the mildest form of autism?

People with **Asperger's syndrome** usually have milder **symptoms** of autistic disorder. They might have social challenges and unusual behaviours and interests. However, they typically do not have problems with language or intellectual disability.

How are Asperger's brains different?

It is correct that the scientific evidence points to the brain of people with autism and Asperger's syndrome as being different but not necessarily "disordered." Studies have shown that the brain in autism develops differently in terms of both structure and function compared with more typical patterns of development and that certain parts of the brain are larger or smaller in people who have autism compared with those who have a more typical brain.

What does a person with Asperger's syndrome often find easy?

People with **Asperger's syndrome** may need more time to process information and **often find** it **easier** to understand clear, consistent language, rather than abstract turns of phrase.

Can someone with Asperger's live independently?

The simple answer to this question is yes, a person with autism spectrum disorder can live independently as an adult.

What are the Signs of autism in children?

Autism in young children

Signs of autism in young children include:

- Not responding to their name

- Avoiding eye contact

- Not smiling when you smile at them

- Getting very upset if they do not like a certain taste, smell or sound

- Repetitive movements, such as flapping their hands, flicking their fingers or rocking their body

- Not talking as much as other children

- Repeating the same phrases

Autism in older children

Signs of autism in older children include:

- Not seeming to understand what others are thinking or feeling

- Finding it hard to say how they feel

- Liking a strict daily routine and getting very upset if it changes

- Having a very keen interest in certain subjects or activities

- Getting very upset if you ask them to do something

- Finding it hard to make friends or preferring to be on their own

- Taking things very literally – for example, they may not understand phrases like "break a leg"

Conclusion

Out of courtesy, we are including a conclusion in book. This is because questions are continually being asked on a daily basis. The above targeted questions may or may not be your priority but desiring to give the best possible answers have been a prime concern.

PART III: Articles on Autism & Asperger's Syndrome

(A) AUTISM ARTICLES:

1. What Causes Autism

Many parents believe that by identifying the cause of autism, the condition may be reversed or avoided. Unfortunately, scientists have yet to identify a single cause of autism in children. It is probable that autism will one day be related to a single gene abnormality, but more likely, the cause is a combination of factors in a child's environment. Since autism cannot be avoided or cured, the most we can do to assist autistic children and adults is to be compassionate and be willing to compromise to make the environment more convenient for them and ourselves.

To begin with, some factors do not cause autism, and these theories must be debunked immediately. Most notably, autism is not caused by poor parenting. Mothers were once criticised for traumatizing their children by cold parenting tactics, which were believed to cause autism. This is just not the case. Autism is often not caused by malnutrition, though food allergies do occur in many autistic children, and some autistic children benefit from daily vitamin supplementation.

There are many connections between autism and the brain. Most autistic people have larger brains that are "wired" differently than the average brain. Since differences exist in multiple areas of the brain, they cannot be attributed to a single brain dysfunction but rather to a brain malfunction in general. Autistic children exhibit symptoms of immune dysfunction as well. The evidence in this study is not yet solid, but research is ongoing. Many autistic people suffer from other health issues linked to immune deficiencies. Overall, these facts seem to point to genetics. While it is not the parents' fault, autism is most likely present elsewhere in your family tree, and it is not unusual for parents to raise more than one autistic child. Autism can also be related to vaccines, though this is still being researched extensively. The benefits of vaccines far outweigh the risks of them causing autism, so you should not deny them to your child simply out of fear. If you have any questions about vaccines, consult your doctor.

Nobody knows for certain what causes autism. As a result, we can do nothing to prevent or cure it; instead, we can only treat autistic people in our lives to the best of our abilities. The key is to educate yourself about autism—the more you know about the condition, the more you will be able to support those who suffer from it. Autism is a complex issue, and as researchers gain new insights into how it affects the body, more medical options will become available, with the expectation that we will one day be able to cure it.

2. The Power of Music - Musical Therapy to Treat Autism

Musical therapy is a relatively recent treatment choice for autistic patients, but it should not be overlooked when considering treatment options. Patients who undergo musical therapy also report significant improvements in temperament and learning abilities. Since music contributes to the nonverbal portion of our minds, it is ideal therapy for conditions where the patient has difficulty communicating, such as autism. If you've been looking for help with autism but haven't had much success in the past, look into this novel treatment process.

Musical therapy is effective because it can be used in combination with social ability growth. Music is a very non-threatening tool for patients, and many games can be played with music to help develop cognitive and behavioural skills. Musical therapy can assist autistic individuals in breaking down social barriers by facilitating eye contact while singing or using instruments that require close proximity to the face.

The most important way musical therapy can benefit children and older autism patients is by assisting in the growth of speech skills. Music helps to bind the brain's verbal and nonverbal functions. Autistic people may have a variety of speech issues. Some people can only hum, grunt, or make other nonverbal sounds, while others babble incoherent words or cries. Others develop the ability to string together phrases and sentences to interact with the rest of the world, though these are normally devoid of feeling. Autistic people are notorious for speaking in monotone tones. However, regardless of how well a person speaks, he or she may engage in musical therapy by clapping patterns, humming along, or singing simple echoing songs.

Autistic people are often exceptionally talented musicians. Some people, for example, have perfect pitch. Others can play a specific instrument very well with little to no guidance. Even if he or she may not demonstrate genius musical talent by conventional standards, an especially difficult autistic person could have musical abilities that surpass his or her other abilities. A musical therapist may use music to connect this type of learning with other types of learning, such as speech development and cognitive behavioural development, as previously mentioned, but also to express emotions and improve memory.

Musical therapy, when used in combination with any of these approaches, will work wonders for autistic people. Music may be used by trained educators to teach children and others how to interact nonverbally, making it easier for patients to understand. Investigate musical therapy as a treatment alternative for you or your child who has autism.

3. Diagnosing Autism & the Role of Physicians

When a doctor first mentions that your child has autism, the first response can be shock and the need to get a second, third, or even fourth opinion. Autism is a difficult condition to identify since each child is unique. However, there are a few key ways for clinicians to reliably diagnose autism in infants, and if your baby or toddler exhibits any of these symptoms of autism, you should promptly contact your pediatrician to express your concerns.

Autism is a condition that develops in a child at a young age, as opposed to a disorder that develops in an older child. It is normally discovered before the age of three, and in many cases, even earlier. Autism commonly manifests itself in the form of delays or deterioration in speech expression. Another early indicator is odd activity in group play and other social settings. A comprehensive physical evaluation and a study of family history by a doctor is the first step in diagnosing autism. While your child's regular pediatrician would be able to detect odd behaviour, you should have your child tested by a specialist who specialises in autism and other related disorders to ensure your child is correctly diagnosed.

Hearing tests are the next step. Language and social ability delays may be caused by a lack of auditory sensations. There are two types of auditory tests: one that tracks the tones a child can hear and one that needs sedation and measures the brain response to specific tones. The first approach is preferred because it does not necessitate the use of sedation. Following auditory examination, your doctor can advise you to have your child tested for Fragile X syndrome, which often co-occurs with autism. Metabolism may also be assessed. Your doctor will require a blood or urine sample to test DNA for this.

An MRI or CAT scan may also aid in the diagnosis of autism. The most important thing is to work with doctors you can rely on. Second opinions can be very useful, but once your child has been diagnosed, stick with one doctor so that care is consistent, and your child becomes used to this individual. Autism is difficult to diagnose and much more difficult to handle, so start learning as much as you can about the condition as soon as your doctor diagnoses it. If you haven't already spoken with your doctor about your child's unusual conduct, do so right away. Early detection of autism gives your child a greater chance of becoming a high-functioning person with many more opportunities in life.

4. Auditory Stimulation: How it Can Help and Hurt an Autistic Child

Since sounds are a part of daily life, among the primary things you should know is how to manage when engaging with an autistic child who seems to have sensory issues, particularly in a classroom environment. For an autistic person, sound may be both harmful and beneficial. Since each autistic person is unique, you should carefully monitor him or her to determine what types of responses to anticipate out of the auditory sensory stimulation.

The most challenging form of sensory stimulus in an autistic child's life can be loud or frightening noises. Several of our everyday activities often include sounds, which impede development. If autistic children are afraid, they cannot and, therefore, will not understand. Parents of autistic children, for example, often report difficulty toilet training their children. This could have been attributed to the frightening sound of the toilet flushing, which could be too much for an autistic child. Rather, consider using a potty seat that is separate from the toilet before they become used to the concept. Foods that are noisy or crunchy are yet another example. If your autistic child is a picky eater, try to identify which foods he or she steadfastly refuses to consume. When food crunches in an autistic child's mouth, it can make a lot of noise, which can damage his or her hearing. If this is really the scenario with your kids, substitute soft foods for crunchy carrots, apples, or potato chips. Other noisy noises, such as a vacuum cleaner, can be damaging to your child's ears. Try to do these things while he or she is not around or suggest giving your child earbuds to use if the world becomes too noisy.

Fixation may also be caused by sounds. Some youngsters, for example, seem to be obsessed with the sights and sounds of lawnmowers. Use this obsession to your advantage. Read stories regarding lawnmowers, for instance, or use humming in combination with a tune. Since sound is a means of nonverbal communication, music is an excellent way for autistic people to learn. This method can be used in learning environments by teachers and parents. The trick is to find a way to make sound work for both you and your kids. Autism is a difficult condition to manage, but by being attentive to your child's individual needs, you can assist him or her in learning to cope with the sounds of daily life.

5. Dealing with Autistic Teenagers – Terrible Teens

With most parents, their child's adolescence is amongst the most difficult times of life. When puberty strikes, young adults' bodies and minds lead to significant changes, and parents have little to no influence over certain cases. Puberty is, therefore, no different in an autistic child. Even though your autistic child cannot go through puberty in the same manner as other children his or her age do, significant hormonal fluctuations do occur in the body. This can have extreme consequences, which can be positive or highly dependent on how your child responds to the new hormone levels.

The occurrence of seizures is among the most frightening side impact of changes in an autistic person's body. Numerous autistic people have seizures from infants to adults, although if your kid does not have these events, he or she can start to have seizures during puberty and afterwards, owing to the body's natural new hormone levels. As odd as it might seem, severe shaking seizures are not really a bad thing. Seizures affect about a quarter of children with autism but often go overlooked because they are not textbook seizures. If you know that your kid is experiencing a seizure, you should take action, and physicians will be able to treat your child more effectively. That being said, if the seizures occur consciously or unconsciously, you and your child might be unaware. These small hidden seizures can lead to a loss of control, which could be tragic, particularly if your child was progressing prior to puberty. Daily check-ups during puberty are also essential.

The adjustments might not be entirely negative. New hormone levels in the body, as well as other adjustments in the onset of puberty, can assist your autistic child in growing and succeeding in areas where he or she previously had no ability or interest. Several parents say that their child's actions changed and also that social interaction became easier.

The most important fact to notice regarding puberty is to know how to closely track your child's shifts and ask your doctor if you have a series of doubts. Note that adolescence is challenging time any young person and would be even more daunting for anyone with autism. Stay patient and compassionate with your teenager and be mindful of regulating his or her autism such that the transition from child to adult is as smooth as possible.

6. "Theory Of Mind" Difficulties - When Lying Isn't a Problem

An autistic person may experience several symptoms; however, one of the most confusing and difficult to comprehend is the recently dubbed Theory of Mind. This issue has been more extensively debated and researched in recent decades, but it remains largely unknown. Because of Theory of Mind issues, social experiences are often more difficult for autistic people.

Theory of Mind contributes to these social behavioural problems in about every context, from playgroups as kids to the social environment as adolescents. Theory of Mind is based on the idea that people with autism struggle to understand that other people around the world hold various perspectives on life. While an autistic child is not necessarily selfish, he or she is likely to believe that everybody thinks, feels, and understands the very same things that he or she does. The majority of people with autism are unable to lie, which isn't really inherently a negative thing but is evidently unnatural. They wouldn't even consider lying because they believe that everyone knows the facts as they see them.

Since people with autism are unable to lie, they are unaware that others are doing so. It is, in truth, a rude awakening for autistic people to discover that others lie or are generally evil. This is particularly unsettling when first encountered in the corporate world, and many people with autism are unsure how and where to deal with it. Since they feel that everybody sees the world the same way they do, they find it difficult to place themselves in the shoes of others. Of course, this can be taught, but it is a difficult process that those with autism must continually consider.

Even children struggle with Theory of Mind; for example, they find it difficult to play games with other children that require them to keep a secret. They often need to be reminded of the importance of sharing and expressing anger in non-harmful ways. Some of an autistic person's anger may derive from their inability to understand why another person is not reacting in the "right" way in a situation. Autistic children often struggle to understand why people don't know those facts—if they know it, everyone else does.

Theory of Mind research is also needed to better understand and treat this autism symptom. Currently, the most effective teaching tool is constant social interaction, as well as role-playing and other activities that enable autistic children to see things from a variety of perspectives. Before medical medicine discovers a better solution to Theory of Mind issues, the best thing to do is be compassionate with autistic people and

7. From School to Work – Smooth Transitions

The move from school to work is one of the most significant in anyone's life. Many people in high school or college live sheltered lives and are also financially and otherwise supported by their parents. These bonds are often severed after graduation, leaving the new graduate to fend for himself or herself. This transition is difficult for everyone, but it is especially difficult for someone with autism. Since school is a time to learn to live with peers in a supervised setting, the workforce is a difficult concept for autistic people to grasp because it requires dealing with new circumstances on a regular basis rather than the security of a fixed living arrangement.

One of the most important things autistic learners must learn is how to interact with others in the business world. This involves good hygiene, which may not have been as essential in high school or college. Brushing your teeth, wearing proper clothes, using deodorant, and combing your hair usually come naturally to most people, but an autistic person requires assistance with these tasks—he or she may be unaware that they are acting inappropriately. At this point in their life, many autistic people who have attended school have reached a degree of maturity in which they can complete the task at hand without difficulty and prevent outbursts, in most cases. In fact, it has been shown that some autistic people are highly skilled at tasks such as math or music. The problem is not learning a new job in the workplace; it is relating to others in a social environment.

Unfortunately, these relationship issues often enable people to take advantage of autistic people. Most autistic people feel that everyone is fundamentally good and similar to them. Unfortunately, it is all too normal in business to come across businesses and business people who do not conduct themselves ethically. This sometimes astounds autistic people, who may have no idea how to manage such a situation. Others in the workplace can also lack the necessary skills to cope with autism, resulting in poor employee relationships. Employers who hire autistic people must not just teach them their new skills, but they must also teach them how to communicate with others.

Pretty much across the board, it is essential for children with autism to understand that there would be a significant difference between life in high school or college and life in the workforce. It is most likely helpful for such people to acquire transition assistance from therapists, relatives, or advisors. It is challenging to transition from school to work, but with just a little inspiration and perseverance, everyone, autistic or not, can progress.

8. Parents Cry for Help: My Child is Autistic but I Don't Know What to Do

Finding out your baby has autism could be a traumatic experience, and sadly, time is short. As a mom, you don't have time to think about why or how this took place; you just have to ponder what to do next. The most important point to know is that you are not struggling alone. You will support your child when coping with your own emotional response by studying the condition and seeking people in similar circumstances.

Join a support network for parents of autistic children. You will locate these by approaching the Autism Society of America. From there, you could find the local branches, most of which have support services for parents and families who have a child who is autistic. Contacting other families in a similar situation could not only make you feel less isolated but can also give you a plethora of support. A parent support network will also find the right doctors, prevention programs, and seminars for your child and your family. Find a support network for any additional children you have. Numerous families overlook the fact that they are not the only ones who must learn to live and interact with their autistic child. You will prevent other children from acting out or against the autistic child by educating them about the condition and locating a support group for them. To better handle your child's illness, you must build a positive atmosphere for the entire family as a parent.

If you are married, you should seek marital therapy. An autistic child can place a serious strain on a marriage, resulting in increasing disputes, disregard of one another, and possibly even accusing one another for the circumstance. Marriage therapy from the start will assist a couple in navigating this discovery and difficult transition, as well as create a more stable atmosphere for your children. Your marriage does not end because you have an autistic child, but the sad reality is that so many do. Prevent this by relying on each other for encouragement and recognizing that you will need assistance in dealing with one another now and in the future.

Most importantly, begin your journey to becoming an expert. Many times, pediatricians or physicians are not autism specialists, which may lead to inaccurate diagnosis or treatment choices. As your child's greatest advocate, you must be well-versed in all aspects of autism. Parents of autistic children may be a valuable resource, and this organisation provides training and seminars. The ASA publishes a newsletter that provides a wealth of knowledge, ranging from diagnosis to treatment. Know, as always, that a support network of parents of autistic children will provide you with books and studies that reflect the facts of the situation. Educate yourself and others around you on what is best for your child—love and guidance.

9. Achieving Self Control with an Autistic Child

Self-discipline is a trait that most children with autism struggle with. This involves unpleasant outbursts and potentially harmful behaviours, such as being abusive against others or posing a threat to themselves by slamming their heads against walls. Self-management is a tool that parents and educators may use to monitor autism impulses and avoid these and many other actions. Giving the child control of himself or herself is always the best way to maintain control in aggressive situations and be a good move toward improving other behaviours.

Self-management operates because the child is no longer fully under the influence of others. Teaching self-control at particular periods of the day, such as when the child is at school or treatment, increases the likelihood that the child will practice self-control during the day. The key is for him or her to have a program in which he or she tracks his or her own actions and activities. Start with short periods of time and progress to more passive monitoring of the child. Every 10 - 15 minutes, inform the individual that he or she is in control and must observe and be mindful of good and bad conduct.

This monitoring functions as a form of self-evaluation. When a child is in command, he or she will reflect more deeply on past and present behaviour. Set specific objectives with the kid, such as an afternoon with no violence against others or a day at school with no self-injury. Every fifteen minutes, check in with the child and see how he or she is doing. Is the objective being met? If the response is no, the child may not be ready for self-management, or the expectations may be too lofty. You want to make sure that the goals are simple at first, and then gradually progress the child to more complex goals in the future. When a child succeeds at self-monitoring, he or she develops a more optimistic attitude toward the experience.

A rewards scheme is, of course, an integral aspect of self-management, allowing the child to choose his or her own reward based on his or her interests. Reinforcement will make these positive behaviour expectations more apparent in the child's mind, and the child will feel completely in charge of the self-management system by selecting and rewarding himself or herself. Start with simple incentives, such as smiley faces for every goal reached and sad faces for every goal not met, and work your way up to a bigger goal, such as a special outing or new toy after a certain number of smiley faces have been achieved.

These systems do not emerge immediately, so make sure you and your child have enough time to commit to a self-management experience. By rewarding good behaviour as dictated by the child rather than an adult, he or she will be more likely to continue even while not engaging in the program. If your autistic child is mature enough, this may be a promising therapeutic option.

10. Dealing with Asperger's Syndrome

Asperger's syndrome is a mild type of autism that affects individuals differently than other forms of autism. Many individuals with autism go untreated because it has little effect on their vocabulary. This is the one type of autism that is not commonly detected at a young age and instead occurs later in life. Asperger's syndrome, on the other hand, may be a very challenging diagnosis to have, so consult your family doctor immediately if you suspect you or your baby of developing communication and social behaviour issues.

Asperger's syndrome has been diagnosed in a number of notable and successful individuals. Historians believe Einstein and Mozart both suffered from this condition. It is important to remember that there are no forms of autism that are associated with mental retardation. In reality, the majority of people with Asperger's syndrome are extremely intelligent. Asperger syndrome does not dictate mental ability; rather, it makes it challenging for people to interact in social environments, similar to how a normal autistic person struggles with group conduct. When this condition goes undiagnosed, children do not receive the necessary treatment, which leads to issues at school, such as bullying. Most children are happy to learn they have Asperger's syndrome rather than believing they are less of a human. By getting diagnosed, you or your child will not only put a name to the issues, but you can also improve the overall condition.

Many of the signs to look out for if you suspect Asperger's syndrome are the same as those experienced by people with full-blown autism. First and foremost, there is social misunderstanding. Many people with Asperger's syndrome have a difficult time dealing with adjustment or change, preferring it to remain constant. A rapidly evolving climate is particularly perplexing. People with Asperger's syndrome may often say rude or disrespectful things when they do not want to, and they may be unable to grasp the thought processes of others. Fixation is another characteristic they share with autistic people, but people with Asperger's syndrome typically have greater control over their fixations, which take the form of intensely concentrated desires. If you think you or a loved one has this condition, here are a few symptoms to look out for. Your doctor should be able to answer any further questions you may have, as well as include reading material and medication for this condition.

11. Dealing with Autism - Finding What Works

When coping with autism, as with any other conditions, you may have many treatment options for yourself or your child. This includes educational, behavioural, medicinal, dietary, and sensory therapies.

Unfortunately, for patients who are not well-off or do not have adequate health insurance, the cost of these services could be higher than they can bear. Monitoring the results of a medication over time is one way to ensure that you or your child receives the best possible treatment for autism. By determining which treatments work and which do not, you will avoid paying for unsuccessful treatments and redirect your resources to those that make a difference.

Before beginning therapy, assess the autistic person's skill. To that end, several programs and organisations, including the Autism Research Institute, offer a checklist of evaluation points that concentrate on autism-related behaviour and illnesses. Autistic people begin to gain functionality as they age, but keep in mind that any of the positive effects of his or her life are actually a result of the normal development process. Fill out the checklist again after two months and equate it to the first. Are there any significant positive changes in behavioural characteristics? If this is the case, it is most likely due to the medication.

It is important to start just one treatment method at a time. If you try all at once, the good and bad effects can balance each other out, and even if the result is completely positive, you won't know which treatment method is causing it and which isn't. Of course, previous research will help you decide which approaches to use, but since autism is such a complex and individual condition, these studies are not always useful. Furthermore, since certain drugs are so recent, research on their long-term effects is normally ineffective. Instead, it is a trial-and-error operation. Two months is sufficient time to investigate the variations of an autistic person undergoing a new therapy. If you do not see good results after two months, you should stop using that form and invest your resources in more effective treatment options.

Remember that you don't necessarily need to wait two months until deciding whether to proceed or discontinue a treatment process. If the side effects of a drug, for example, are messing with the patient's life in an unbearable manner, the procedure should be stopped. You can also make ongoing treatments based on immediate positive responses—just remember to keep track of the various methods. Autistic people, like anyone else, develop and age, so therapies can no longer be effective after a certain period of time. Consult your doctor before doing something new to ensure that you are as safe and secure as possible.

12. Bad Apples in the Family Tree

The discovery that a child in the family is autistic is often met with a variety of reactions. While in a perfect world, all family members, including extended family members, will be supportive, the sad reality is that many are disgusted or disappointed. Is the autistic child often chastised by a family member? Does he or she treat your autistic child unfairly? Is this family member adamant about treating your autistic child the same way he or she treats all of your other children, even when it is inappropriate? There are indications that this parent is not interested in your autistic child or the situation. This is always the case when a child is diagnosed with autism, so as a parent, be conscious and prepared for this to occur.

Unreceptive relatives also do not grasp autism or what it means for your child and your immediate family. While many people associate autism with mental retardation, many autistic children and adults are extremely intelligent; they are simply unable to articulate this in the same manner as others can. Try explaining autism to this family member and inviting him or her to spend time with you and your autistic child. Allow them to see the symptoms of autism and the coping strategies you may use.

If the family member is unsupportive or refuses to listen to your clarification, inquire why this family member is so resistant to the situation. Are they afraid of injuring the child? Are they concerned about the additional responsibilities that come with spending time with the child? Perhaps they feel guilty or humiliated. If you can figure out why a family member is being resistant, you can better fix the problem and potentially help him or her resolve their preconceived notions.

Perhaps no amount of conversation or spending time with this family member can help them overcome their prejudice. If this person is adamant, you will never be able to show him or her how beautiful your son or daughter is, autism and all. If this is the case, removing this person from your life would be difficult, but it will also free you and your child from this family member's negative energy and personality. In this evolving scenario, you need the most constructive assistance possible. Remember that other family members have been helpful and that your children are adapting well and providing you with strength. Participate in parent support groups for autistic children to expand the support network. And keep in mind that you can choose whether to surround yourself with people who support and love your child-family or not.

13. Autistic Child: Forms of Teaching and Tolerance

Understanding how children with autism learn is essential for educating them with the same zeal as other children. This may appear to be a simple concept, but children with autism learn in such a unique way that understanding autism is essential when teaching autistic children. Teachers can better learn to work with autistic children and adults both in and out of the classroom by being knowledgeable about the disease, resulting in a more accepting world for all.

Visual thinkers are common in autistic children. As a result, teaching by speaking would be ineffective. For the autistic child to completely comprehend the lesson, teachers should mix pictures and vocabulary. For example, if you're talking about animals around the world, you should have a flashcard with the word "mouse," say it slowly and clearly, and show the child a picture of a mouse. Bring in a live mouse for display and discussion. Since verbs require action and may be more difficult to illustrate, nouns can be easier to teach autistic children. When teaching autistic children terms like "sit" or "stand," you should complete these acts as well. Furthermore, because of their visual nature, autistic children often struggle to understand long sentences. They become perplexed because they are unable to decode the series. Writing instructions may thus be extremely useful when proctoring exams or quizzes.

As visual thinkers, autistic children often fixate on a specific object or image. If this is the case, consider integrating the object or image into lesson plans. If the child enjoys planes, try to incorporate planes as visuals into the lesson as much as possible. For example, when teaching math, make word problems about planes to keep the child's attention. Autistic children are often more likely to be creative or musical, with exceptionally original drawings and above-average skill with instruments or voice. Set aside time during the day for the arts and allow children to participate in activities they enjoy.

Because of their lack of control over their hands and movement, autistic children can have difficulty writing. This is a source of frustration for both the child and the teacher. Enable the child to use a computer to relieve frustration. If you can, make sure the keyboard and monitor are close together because the child will have trouble recalling what he or she has recently typed.

By being willing to educate an autistic child to the best of your abilities, you are not only providing the best opportunity for him or her in life, but you are also serving as a positive role model for the other children in the class. Allowing an autistic child to ruin the learning experience for others is unacceptable; instead, integrate his or her peculiarities into the lessons as much as possible. The best gift you can give this child is a more prejudice-free classroom.

B. Asperger's Syndrome Articles

1. What exactly is Asperger's Syndrome?

Asperger's syndrome, also known as Asperger disorder, is a type of autism. It is a permanent impairment that affects how a person processes information from the outside world and interacts with others. Because of the number of ways in which it affects others, autism is often referred to as a "spectrum disorder." Asperger's syndrome is one of the pieces of the puzzle.

Individuals with Asperger's syndrome also have average or above-normal intelligence and language development, but they often exhibit autistic-like tendencies and significant deficits in social and communication skills. Hans Asperger, a Viennese psychiatrist, named the condition after publishing a paper explaining a pattern of behaviours in 1944. Despite the publication, the condition was not applied to the DSM-IV until 1994, and it has only recently been recognised by practitioners and parents.

Individuals with Asperger's syndrome have a normal IQ and possibly extraordinary ability or talent in a particular field. These people are often regarded as eccentric and are frequently the targets of ridicule and bullying. Their language learning seems average on the surface, but they frequently have pragmatic deficits. This indicates that they have trouble comprehending the intended sense of speech.

People with Asperger's syndrome were once thought to have a secret disability. This suggested that an outsider would not understand their situation unless they might work in society. They do, however, struggle with social contact, social interaction, and social imagination. If they don't have the learning disorders associated with autism, they may have dyslexia, dyspraxia, or ADHD.

Individuals with Asperger's syndrome have trouble expressing themselves emotionally and socially, as well as interpreting facial gestures and differentiating tone of voice. They struggle with knowing when to start and end a conversation, as well as how to use complicated terms and phrases. Individuals always want to be social but fail to initiate social relationships and can struggle to form and sustain friendships. Individuals with Asperger's syndrome do not understand social norms, which most people learn without thought at a young age. They perceive others to be unpredictable and perplexing, and as a result, they can withdraw and appear uninterested in others.

While people can be extremely innovative and inventive as accomplished authors, artists, and musicians, they can also struggle with social imagination. This means they have difficulty predicting the results of events or interpreting other people's thoughts or feelings conveyed by facial expressions and body language.

Other similar characteristics include finding comfort in routines and having an extreme, if not obsessive, interest in a particular hobby or set. Some people experience sensory problems, which can affect one or more of their senses. The degree of complexity varies from person to person, but the most common way is a feeling that is either overdeveloped or underdeveloped. Bright lights or noisy sounds, for example, can cause anxiety or pain in someone with Asperger's syndrome.

Researchers discovered structural and functional variations in particular regions of the brain using sophisticated brain imaging techniques. These variations are most likely the result of irregular embryonic cell migration during development when the child is still in the womb. A number of studies have found variations in brain function when Asperger's syndrome children are asked to respond to particular tasks. While researchers believe there is a genetic component since Asperger syndrome tends to run in families, further evidence is required to establish a connection between genetic mutations and Asperger's syndrome.

2. Behaviour of Children with Asperger's Syndrome – Part 1 of 3

Children with Asperger's syndrome possess unique behavioural patterns that can make life complicated for them at home and school. In the early 1940s, Hans Asperger, a Viennese pediatrician, was the first one to record a collection of traits, widely known as Asperger's syndrome. He encountered a bunch of kids with the disorder, who had varying levels of intelligence and learning skills but seemed to struggle with communication and socialization.

It took until the mid-1990s for psychiatry to understand the condition in the DSM-IV, and much longer for physicians and parents to comprehend the disorder of Asperger's syndrome.

Asperger's syndrome is classified as an autism spectrum disorder or a chronic personality disorder. Since it is one of many on this continuum, and because Asperger's syndrome presents in many different ways, children do not exhibit precisely the same list of conditions but may exhibit behavioural similarities. Because of these difficulties, diagnosing kids with Asperger's syndrome can be difficult. Some researchers may use a number of terms, such as autism or high functioning autism, both of which have problems related to Asperger's syndrome.

What distinguishes Asperger's syndrome from autism is that autistic behaviour appears far earlier in life than Asperger's syndrome. Asperger's syndrome appears when an infant is well past the age of three, with the majority of symptoms happening between the ages of five and nine. Children with autism are often identified before the age of two.

Children with Asperger's syndrome can display symptoms, including an inability to interact with others or develop intense fixations on items. These obsessive fixations may be mistaken for obsessive-compulsive disorder, which really is one condition that is mistaken for Asperger's syndrome.

Children can even grow strange speech patterns and even strange movements. These habits may be the product of cognitive deficits, which are the cause of their Asperger's syndrome. They are often not vocal and find it difficult to understand nonverbal contact from others. Because of the combination of these two traits, children are often singled out as targets for bullies and teasing. Some other children conclude that these children are self-centered, arrogant, or egotistical because they are unable to engage in social contact because they are unable to.

Children with Asperger's syndrome are often known to be hypersensitive to some sensory triggers. Contact, sound, and light are examples of these. Fluorescent tube lighting can cause them to avert their eyes and position their hands over their ears in response to noises that many others feel soothing. These activities in children with Asperger's syndrome limit their capacity to interact in normal society as well as improve their social isolation due to social immaturity, weirdness, or even forgetfulness.

Children would have little contact with others, not because they'd rather, but because they are unwilling to communicate in a social environment that involves the other person. They respond to other children in society that are inconsistent with the social situation.

A person with ASD will have delayed language growth, while children with Asperger's syndrome will also have outstanding grammar skills as well as a large vocabulary. They may, however, read nonverbal cues in communication and misinterpret most humor.

Children can grow normally in terms of being able to dress, support themselves, and feed themselves; however, they would be unable to have a "natural" memory span and will have very limited organisational abilities.

3. Behaviour of Children with Asperger's Syndrome – Part 2 of 3

Children with Asperger's syndrome tend to have no rational thinking, particularly as they get older. That's because they view the world surrounding them in a definitive manner and lack social creativity. A child should be able to use social imagination to perceive humor, non-verbal social communication skills, and finish another person's sentence when they understand the entire situation. Those activities would be impossible for kids with Asperger's syndrome to complete.

Kids with Asperger's syndrome may also be inconsistent in their ability to engage in, give and take social interactions. Even if the child may facilitate interactions, they are usually considered to be "on his own terms." From the outside, these children seem rather egocentric and may be solely concerned with their own wishes, needs, and desires. They can appear quiet or withdrawn at times, with little social drive. This means they can't communicate with other children their own age due to fear of rejection or the seriousness of the disorder.

Therefore, these children cannot learn social codes. They do not learn by observation or repeated verbal reminders. They do not deliberately disregard or violate the rules, but they have a tough time correctly interpreting their social environment and do not realise why a specific rule applies to a specific social event. An instructor, for example, should remind a child with Asperger's syndrome that he cannot force other children. He may be reminded before leaving for recess, but once outside, the child may push several other children.

4. Behaviour of Children with Asperger's Syndrome – Part 3 of 3

Some children and adolescents have clothing preferences based on their level of comfort or sensory sensitivity. Children rarely make clothing choices based on peer pressure, but rather on concerns about their own comfort. Some children, for example, prefer no ridges on the neck, no elastic at the waist or wrist, and no buttons down the front of his shirt. Others prefer blue jeans, while others only wear elastic waist trousers.

Their lack of social creativity and communication skills would also make it difficult for them to learn, read, and solve problems. These children would also show clumsy and uncoordinated body movements, making them a focus for teasing in gym class and bad choices for athletic events.

Although highly articulate and expressive language skills can persuade others that the child has advanced communication skills, this is a mislabeling of the child's abilities. Children can struggle with narrative skills, such as relating past events or retelling stories or television shows in a sequential manner. They sometimes leave out crucial pieces of relevant information and can fully rewrite the story.

Asperger's syndrome children have the intelligence and language development to work in a typical classroom. On the other hand, their peers and classmates should be informed of their condition-related unique behavioural mannerisms and learning abilities. It should be remembered that prior to any peer training, the parent of the child with Asperger's syndrome must give permission. This exchange of knowledge with the child's classmates, especially when children discover that the child with Asperger's syndrome does not want to behave in these ways and is unable to work in any other way, also contributes to greater understanding and social acceptance by their peers.

Although the actions of children with Asperger's syndrome may present a major challenge to parents, peers, and teachers, there are unique techniques that can be used to promote more positive engagement for the children, as well as social strategies that can benefit them throughout their lives.

5. Diagnosis of Asperger's Syndrome

Hans Asperger, a Viennese pediatrician, was the first to characterise Asperger's syndrome. In 1944, he published a paper describing a series of patterns he discovered in some of his patients. He observed that while the boys' intellect and language learning were average, they had significantly impaired social skills and were unable to communicate effectively with others.

It took until 1994 for the diagnosis of Asperger's syndrome to be added to the DSM-IV, and even then, many professionals thought it was one of several spectrum disorders. Asperger's syndrome is distinguished by a lack of social skills, obsessions, and unusual speech patterns. Unfortunately, these traits make these people the object of constant bullying and the brunt of the class bully.

Individuals with Asperger's syndrome often have few facial expressions and can struggle to read the body language of others. Parents would complain that their children engaged in obsessive routines, often becoming completely engrossed in a hobby or set. Children and adults also exhibit unusual sensitivity to various stimuli, whether that be touch, smell, taste, or sight. Individuals, for example, may be distracted by a light that no one else sees and may cover their ears to block out sounds. Others may find clothing to be constricting and opt for items made of specific materials or lacking elastic at the wrist and ankle.

Individuals with Asperger's syndrome are generally capable of living and holding down a stable career. They are, however, socially unstable and often labeled as strange or eccentric.

Parents and significant others can note some motor delays or clumsiness in the individual's ability to work as well. Adults will always struggle to show empathy for others, and social situations will always be challenging.

Asperger's syndrome diagnosis can be complicated, and misdiagnoses are common. This is complicated further because many of the same symptoms present in people with Asperger's are also found in people with other conditions.

6. What is Asperger's Disability Spectrum?

Asperger's syndrome is classified as one of the autism spectrum disorders or personality pervasive disorders (an older description). It is almost always viewed as a major functioning type of autism since these individuals have normal or above-average intelligence and academic skills.

Persons with Asperger's syndrome would have more trouble interacting with one another and will exhibit a slew of symptoms, such as low social creativity, poor social contact, and poor verbal interaction. In certain situations, they are often unable to make eye contact and, therefore, do not read and respond to social signals in the same way most of us do instinctively.

Some argue that Asperger's syndrome is not a disorder at all but rather a disparity in ability. The truth is that a lot of people who have the signs still have unique talents that should not be overlooked. These abilities are often seen in math or music. This is not to be confused with an autistic person, but rather with someone who has a highly established ability or talent and is called a savant.

The distinction is due to the individual's level of language development and intellect. Individuals with Asperger's syndrome have the potential to become really active functioning members of society if the proper measures are taken to assist them in finding solutions and protective factors to try to resolve their symptoms.

There is no accepted treatment for the signs and disease of Asperger's syndrome. Researchers now conclude that it is the product of a developmental imbalance in the brain, which presents itself with difficulty in social relationships. Individual people should learn to build coping mechanisms to help them communicate with society and reduce their stress level because the operation and brain structure cannot be modified.

Individuals with Asperger's syndrome do have a wide range of activities and disabilities. Some have almost the same behaviour issues as those with autism, whereas others tend to be comfortable in social settings and have only slight obsessive-compulsive behaviours or ritualistic conduct.

Frustration kicks in for both the person and their family members whenever the sufferer refuses to seek treatment because they cannot see the future or have any optimism for the future.

Asperger's syndrome is typically diagnosed in infancy after the age of three, while autism is usually diagnosed before the age of three. There is no guarantee of the future for those who suffer from the effects of Asperger's syndrome, but it has been discovered that individual therapy to help individuals develop coping mechanisms and family counseling to help family members deal with non-intentional activities is the best solution to improve an individual's ability to work in society.

Following an Asperger's syndrome diagnosis, family members and parents often wonder what the future holds for their child and sibling. Unfortunately, because of the wide variety of disabilities that a person can encounter during their lifetime, doctors and psychologists are unable to provide an accurate image of what the future will look like. All that can be guaranteed is that their family member will now be able to access care and services that were not previously available prior to 1994, when the condition was first entered into the DSM-IV. While this is small consolation, studies into the causes and therapies that can benefit people with Asperger's syndrome or high functioning autism continues.

7. Research Therapy - Asperger's syndrome

Asperger's syndrome is a developmental condition that mainly affects a child's communication and socialization skills. Children with Asperger's syndrome have a lot of difficulty in social situations. They notably concentrate on particular subjects and try to learn everything they can about them. It is a neurological condition that is classified as part of the autism spectrum disorder family, also known as pervasive developmental disorders. Asperger's syndrome is a milder form of autism spectrum disorder.

Children with Asperger's syndrome can avoid making eye contact with others, make awkward body movements and gestures, and show little facial expression. They enjoy focusing on one subject and talking about it. They have difficulty reading other people's facial expressions and nonverbal communication. Children with Asperger's syndrome can have impaired coordination and speak in a monotone or rapid manner. Asperger's symptoms may be mistaken for normal childhood growth. When a child has difficulty adjusting to social situations, it is time to seek outside intervention and meet with your child's pediatrician.

Asperger's syndrome is considered to be a neurological disorder that cannot be treated. However, through counseling, children and adults can learn to deal with their symptoms and engage socially with others. Medication, such as those used to treat ADHD, may be beneficial to certain adolescents.

The hormone oxytocin, which exists naturally in humans, is currently being used in research to treat Asperger's syndrome and autism. This hormone is thought to improve people's social sensitivity and response capacities when communicating with others and coping with their emotions.

It's unclear how oxytocin functions in this case. However, it is believed to promote bonding in relationships and is secreted in a woman's body during orgasm, pregnancy, and breastfeeding. This research was previously conducted in humans and revealed important abilities in interpreting the expressions of others. Expectations are high, and research is being carried out on male subjects in their early to late adolescent years using an oxytocin nasal spray. This test will be carried out for a year, after which a follow-up will be carried out.

8. Autism or Asperger's Syndrome?

Because of how autism can manifest itself in different people, it is sometimes referred to as a spectrum disorder. There is no single known cause, and given the disease's complexity and the fact that no two children are identical, it is very likely that there are many causes. At this stage, researchers conclude that these causes may include genetic errors, environmental factors, the function of the immune system, and birth-related brain injury.

The controversial correlation between autism and certain childhood vaccinations, especially the measles-mumps-rubella vaccine, is one of the most contentious issues surrounding the disease. Others also attributed autism to vaccines that contain thimerosal, a mercury-containing preservative. Many scientists and doctors agree that most children's vaccines have been thimerosal-free since 2001. However, this preservative is still present in the flu vaccine. Extensive research has now been conducted that has neither proved nor disproven the correlation between autism and vaccines.

Asperger's syndrome is a disorder that exists on the autism spectrum. Individuals with this disorder have normal intelligence and language development, as well as none of the learning disorders typically associated with autism, but they do have some of the behavioural signs that are commonly associated with autism.

Children with Asperger's syndrome typically exhibit a triad of symptoms, including difficulties with social communication, social imagination, and social interaction. Children and adults with Asperger's syndrome usually have an all-consuming interest in a specific subject or hobby.

Researchers classify Asperger's syndrome as part of a group of conditions known as autism spectrum disorders or pervasive developmental disorders (older term). All of these include difficulties with social skills and speech, while Asperger's syndrome is considered to be on the milder end of the continuum.

In fact, Asperger's syndrome was so mild that despite being identified in the literature as early as 1944, it wasn't included in the DSM-IV until 1994, and much later until professionals and parents understood it. Individuals with Asperger's syndrome were previously thought to be quirky or unusual but did not have a diagnosis or were considered impaired.

Controversy surrounds Asperger's syndrome because experts are still debating whether high functioning Asperger's syndrome is really a disorder or merely a "difference." They believe that by classifying this disorder as different, the diagnosis would be more neutral and value-free than if it were defined as an illness or a disability. The above can only refer to lower functioning cases of autism and should be reserved for those who need financial and physical assistance.

Individuals with Asperger's syndrome and autism have a difficult disorder that causes them to be socially withdrawn and lonely. The disease, by definition, causes problems in socialisation and communication for both the child and the parents. When a child's meltdown is caused by a disability rather than "poor parenting," it usually means less play dates, birthday invites, and looks from parents in public.

Asperger's syndrome and autism are also symptoms of pervasive personality disorder or autism spectrum disorder, but they are at opposite ends of the spectrum. At this time, researchers are trying to discover the cause of both disorders, as well as improved care protocols and the likelihood of prevention.

9. Resources for Adults with Asperger's Syndrome

Asperger's disease, also known as high functioning autism, is a moderate type of autism. This is a psychological condition that impairs one's ability to communicate and connect with others in social situations. A child with Asperger's syndrome will often avoid eye contact, make awkward expressions and gestures, and concentrate on one or two particular subjects, learning everything they can about them.

Individuals with Asperger's syndrome are intelligent and have normal language growth. They do, however, exhibit other behavioural anomalies and struggle with social contact. Both children and adults have difficulty 'reading' nonverbal communication and facial expressions.

The precise cause of Asperger's syndrome is unclear at this time, but scientists believe genetics plays a significant role in the condition's growth. With therapies and medication to help with social interaction, a child with Asperger's syndrome can lead a very normal life. Treatment may be beneficial, so it is best to start as soon as possible.

Adults with Asperger's syndrome are not developmentally disabled; in fact, they are often highly intelligent and regarded as rational and deep thinkers. Many celebrities, including Keanu Reeves, Woody Allen, Bill Gates, Al Gore, and Bob Dylan, are accused of having Asperger's syndrome. Asperger's syndrome has little regard for social or ethnic distinctions. It is worth noting, however, that it is three to four times more common in men than women.

Adults with Asperger's syndrome can find the best resources through the National Autistic Society, where Asperger's, a high functioning type of autism, is also discussed, as well as helpful statistics, local organisations, and website links relating to this psychological condition. There are also support groups for Asperger's syndrome families, both for the infant and the adult sufferer.

Parents may be unable to identify Asperger's-related variations in their young children because these differences are still common behaviours in children. Parents, on the other hand, notice subtle variations between siblings. A diagnosis can be ignored or misdiagnosed as ADHD. Sometimes, a diagnosis is not made until later in life, or even by the Asperger's sufferer themselves in their early adult years. Adult Asperger's syndrome sufferers may say that they simply felt different and that their thought processes were not the same as those of their peers.

For more information and services for adults with Asperger's syndrome, contact your local Autism community or conduct an online web search for additional Asperger's syndrome support groups.

10. Resources for Children with Asperger's Syndrome

Asperger's syndrome children also pose a challenge to educators in the school system and to their parents if they are homeschooled. These children frequently seem competent because they have normal intelligence and language development. Children with Asperger's syndrome typically excel at memorization and objective knowledge but struggle with comprehension.

Families with children who exhibit signs of high functioning autism, also known as Asperger's syndrome, often face the additional responsibility of providing their children with services and help both outside and within the school system.

Children's treatment protocols include improving their social and communication skills so that they can articulate themselves better, understand words, and interact with others. Both these factors increase the probability of good encounters, which affects their ability to have long-term relationships, succeed in their careers, and maintain friendships.

There are currently very few services explicitly tailored to solve the concerns of children with Asperger's syndrome. Any treatment interventions used by adults with high functioning autism may also be effective for children with Asperger's syndrome.

Families who see their children's trials benefit from counseling and other services to help their children, themselves, and the rest of the family. Individuals with Asperger's syndrome may join networking organisations. These groups are often identified by looking through local databases or contacting local hospital social workers, who have extensive lists of neighborhood social service programs.

Families can also communicate with other families online via forums and chat groups. The majority of these groups are designed to assist families in finding the right support in their neighborhoods and among themselves so that they can be the best parents possible for children who face a range of challenges.

11. Screening for Asperger's Syndrome

Asperger's syndrome is classified as a moderate spectrum disorder or pervasive personality disorder. Asperger's syndrome is linked to autism because of its symptoms and diagnostic criteria. It was sometimes referred to as a "silent disorder" since it was not recognised in the DSM-IV until after 1994, and it was even later before doctors and parents recognised the disease.

Some consider Asperger's syndrome to be a developmental disorder since the majority of people have normal intelligence and language development, but social interaction falls short. At this time, there is no single definitive diagnostic test that can be used to decide whether a person has Asperger's syndrome. Instead, the physician, a child's instructor, and the parents collaborate on diagnosis and testing. A counselor may be called on at times to assess peer relationships, responses to new circumstances, and the ability to recognise emotions or other forms of indirect communication.

Individual tasks that help to point sufferers in the direction of a possible diagnosis have been developed to increase social understanding of people who suffer from Asperger's syndrome, and, therefore, acceptance of these individuals. Although these assessments are often available on the internet, they may not be entirely accurate. However, they do assist with pointing individuals in the right direction in order to figure out how to deal with their social situation.

These online assessments are more accurate in adult contexts than pediatric settings. In other words, the majority of them are intended to raise questions about adult behaviours rather than those encountered in the classroom. An assessment with their primary care provider, a counselor, and the help of their parents is best for them. Children who grow up with this condition are more likely to be bullied and subjected to cruel bullying by their peers.

Children are more vulnerable because those with Asperger's syndrome cannot communicate socially with their peers in the same way that their classmates do. Individuals with Asperger's syndrome often struggle with social communication, social interaction, and social imagination. This simply means that, despite having normal or above-average intelligence and normal language learning, these children are often unable to engage in social contact with their peers, making them targets for bullying.

http://www.piepalace.ca/blog/asperger-test-aq-test is an online Asperger's syndrome quiz that can help people assess their risk factor for this diagnosis.

Adults with Asperger's syndrome find it difficult to understand small-talking interactions and would rather sit with a machine than with an adult. When adults seek a diagnosis from their doctor, the testing normally begins with an IQ exam.

For high-functioning expressive young adults, doctors can also prescribe an autism screening observation plan. Both assessments allow a doctor to examine a patient's social communication skills and actions.

Online assessments should never be used to replace a diagnosis made by a licensed physician or psychiatrist.

12. Treatment of Asperger's Syndrome

Asperger syndrome is a neurobiological disorder that may affect both children and adults. Many people believe it is a type of high functioning autism, and it is classified as a spectrum disorder or widespread personality disorder. It has an impact on a person's ability to socialise and interact effectively with others. Individuals also show signs of social contact, social interaction, and social creativity.

At the moment, physicians and researchers have not discovered a cause or cure for Asperger's syndrome. Some evidence suggests that people with this disorder have irreversible changes to their frontal lobe. These modifications affect the brain's ability to process social interactions.

In 1944, Hans Asperger coined the term "autistic psychopathy" and published a paper explaining the signs and behaviours. However, the disability was not recognised in the DSM-IV until 1994. Despite the many various scientific studies that have been conducted over the years, the precise cause of this disease has never been determined.

Although there is no cure for Asperger's syndrome at the moment, there are treatment protocols that can help both adults and children learn how to communicate more effectively in social settings. The prescribed treatment is based on the individual's level of adaptive functioning. Individuals with Asperger's syndrome, like those with autism, have a wide spectrum of impairment or functionality.

Communication and social skills preparation are available resources for children and adults with Asperger's syndrome to help people understand the unwritten laws of socialisation and communication. In the same way, these are often too complex for youngsters. This is because mastering these social communication skills is like learning a foreign language for children and adults with Asperger's syndrome.

It is possible for children with Asperger syndrome to learn how to communicate in a more normal rhythm, as well as how to interpret speech cues such as movements, eye contact, tone of voice, humor, and sarcasm that normally fly right over their heads.

Cognitive behaviour therapy is another form of behavioural therapy that may be prescribed. This approach aims to reduce problem habits like interrupting, obsessions, and angry outbursts. They also concentrate on assisting children and adults in recognising a troubled environment, such as a new location or activities, and then selecting a particular coping plan.

Although there is no drug explicitly designed to treat Asperger's syndrome, certain symptoms, such as anxiety, depression, or hyperactivity, can be managed with medication. To address these issues, generally selective serotonin reuptake inhibitors, antipsychotics, and certain stimulants are used.

Individuals with Asperger's syndrome typically have a high correlation between their treatment outlook and their assessed IQ. Those with higher IQs would do better and show greater gains in social function than those with lower IQs.

Children who exhibit Asperger's syndrome symptoms will also need some help in the school system. Schools with a communications teacher who is interested in social skills instruction, opportunities for social interaction and organised environments, a concern for teaching real-life skills, and a desire to individualise the program are ideally suited to support people with Asperger's syndrome. Parents should keep up to date with what is going on in their child's classroom and communicate with the teacher on a regular basis.

Even though there is no clear pill for Asperger's syndrome treatment and no cure, people with this disorder will adjust to their surroundings if they are taught coping mechanisms and have a strong support network in their relationships.

PART IV

ALL BOOKS PUBLISHED
BY AUTHOR OF THIS BOOK

BOOKS ON CREATION & EVOLUTION

BOOKS ON WELLNESS & HEALTH

10

11

12

13

14

BOOKS ON ALZHEIMER'S & DEMENTIA

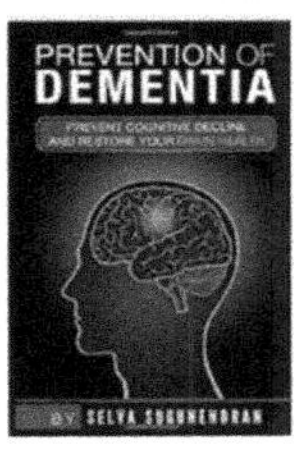
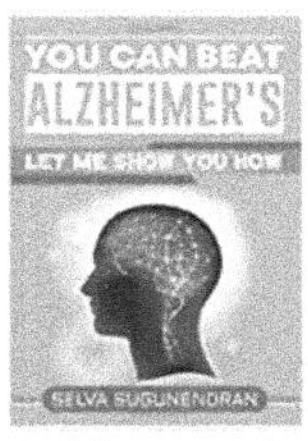

BOOKS ON SUCCESS

References

1. *The Survival Guide for Kids with Autism Spectrum Disorders (And Their Parents) by Elizabeth Verdick and Elizabeth Reeve M.D.*

2. *https://www.webmd.com/brain/autism/how-do-doctors-diagnose-autism*

3. *https://www.healthline.com/health/fragile-x-syndrome#causes*

4. *https://molecularautism.biomedcentral.com/articles/10.1186/2040-2392-3-5*

5. *https://health.howstuffworks.com/pregnancy-and-parenting/baby-health/special-needs/10-causes-of-low-birth-weight4.htm*

6. *https://www.ncbi.nlm.nih.gov/pmc/articles/PMC4511955/*

7. *https://www.healthline.com/health/aspergers-symptoms-in-adults*

8. *A Comprehensive book on Autism Spectrum Disorders by Mohammad-Reza Mohammadi*

9. *Remedy Health Media (https://www.psycom.net/autism-famous-people)*

10. *https://allthatsinteresting.com/famous-people-with-autism*

11. *https://www.wikihow.com/Treat-Autism*

12. *http://www.cdc.gov/ncbddd/autism/index.htm*

13. *http://autism.about.com/od/alternativetreatmens/f/rpm.htm*

14. *http://www.rdiconnect.com/about-rdi/*

15. *http://www.sentex.net/~nexus23/naa_aba.html*

16. *http://juststimming.wordpress.com/2011/10/05/quiet-hands/*

17. *http://www.webmd.com/brain/news/20050826/boy-dies-after-controversial-treatment-for-autism*

18. *http://www.bbc.com/news/uk-england-london-33079776*

19. https://restlesshands42.wordpress.com/2016/02/19/and-yet-again-aba-whats-wrong-with-it-and-what-can-be-changed/

20. http://michellesuttonwrites.com/2015/11/16/the-letter-i-wish-i-had-read-when-my-children-were-diagnosed-with-autism/

21. http://www.thinkingautismguide.com/2014/02/do-me-favor.html

22. http://www.thinkingautismguide.com/2014/10/dr-jonine-biesman-avoiding-crises.html

23. http://www.buzzfeed.com/bradesposito/letter-viral-aus#.imyDXKperQ

24. http://autisticadvocacy.org/2012/06/you-are-not-a-burden/

25. https://www.sciencedaily.com/releases/2020/04